# Dramatic Mark

*St Mark's Gospel arranged for Performance*

# Dramatic Mark

*St Mark's Gospel arranged for Performance*

Christopher Bryan

**DIAMOND PRESS**

*Dramatic Mark: St Mark's Gospel Arranged for Dramatic Performance*
Christopher Bryan

© 2025 Christopher Bryan. All rights reserved. No part of this book may be used or reproduced in any manner whatsoever without written permission except in the case of brief quotations embodied in critical articles and reviews.

Permission for any kind of public performance must be obtained from the author. For amateur productions, this permission will normally be granted without charge, with the proviso only that said permission is acknowledged in the programme or any other publicity associated with the production.

Edition ISBNs:
Trade Paperback: ISBN 978-0-9978496-5-3
e-book: ISBN: 978-0-9978496-6-0

First Edition 2025

Copy Editor: Vicki Burgess

Cover design: Kara Kosaka

Book Design and Production: Topics –The Creative Partnership Limited, Exeter, UK

Typset in 11/14 Bodoni 72 Old Style

Photograph of Christopher Bryan by Wendy Bryan

*For David Landon,*
*who taught me to love*
*theatre in general*
*and Shakespeare in particular,*
*with affection and gratitude.*

# Contents

## Introduction

| | |
|---|---:|
| The Origins of Mark's Gospel | 9 |
| Mark's Gospel and Performance | 12 |
| The Language of Mark's Gospel | 13 |
| The Conclusion to Mark's Gospel | 15 |
| Performing *Dramatic Mark* | 18 |

## Dramatic Mark

| | |
|---|---:|
| Prelude | 23 |
| Prologue | 25 |
| Act 1 | 27 |
| Act 2 | 61 |
| Act 3 | 75 |
| Epilogue | 104 |

Select Bibliography     107

# Introduction

## The Origins of Mark's Gospel

At some time during the first Christian century a follower of Jesus of Nazareth decided to write what his contemporaries would have called a "Life" (Greek: *bios*, Latin, *vita*) of his Lord.[1] Its purpose, in common with most such "Lives" of the period (and it was a popular genre) was mainly what they would have called "epideictic" (that is, celebrating and honouring its subject) and to some extent "deliberative" (that is, inviting those who heard it to behave in a way appropriate for his admirers). The result was what we now know as the Gospel according to St Mark.

Who was this creative person? He himself does not tell us, perhaps, as has been suggested, out of modesty. But whether or not that was the case, others certainly *were* interested in who he was. As early as within two or three decades of its publication, people were attributing the gospel to John Mark, son of that Mary (not, of course, the mother of Our Lord) whose house in Jerusalem was a meeting place for Christians from the earliest days of the church.[2] Mark is a figure otherwise on the fringes of early Christian history—variously spoken of here and there in the New Testament as "cousin" to

---

[1] See, seminally, Richard A. Burridge, *What Are the Gospels?: A Comparison with Graeco-Roman Biography* (Waco, Texas: Baylor University 2018 [Cambridge University, 1992]); also my own *Preface to Mark: Notes on the Gospel in Its Literary and Cultural Settings* (Oxford University, 1993).
[2] Acts 12.12.

# Dramatic Mark: The Gospel according to St Mark

Barnabas, as Paul's fellow worker (not always harmoniously—at one point Paul fired him!), and as a "son" to Peter.³ Slightly later tradition goes on to speak of him as "Peter's interpreter,"⁴ and congruent with that his gospel does indeed contain reminiscences, such as the account of Peter's denial, that seem likely to have come from the Apostle himself. It has been suggested that an odd little anecdote in the middle of the passion story about a boy who followed the disciples to Gethsemane and then at the time of Jesus' arrest had to run home naked⁵ might be Mark's own little "signature", and although many commentators (by no means all) reject the idea, it seems to me not all unlikely. Such a strange and apparently inconsequential addition to the narrative must have been inserted for some reason, and the "signature" theory is as plausible as any other I have seen, and rather more so than some.⁶

---

³ Acts 12.25, 15.37-39; Col. 4.10; 2 Tim. 4.11; Philem. 1.24; 1 Pet. 5.13.

⁴ Eusebius cites Papias, bishop of Hierapolis, probably writing around AD 95-110, in turn citing an earlier (and unknown) "John the Presbyter": "Mark became Peter's interpreter and wrote down accurately, but not in order, all that he remembered of the things said and done by the Lord." Eusebius makes the point that though Papias did not himself know the apostles, he was in direct contact with those who had heard them, including John the Elder, Aristion, Polycarp, and the daughters of Philip the Evangelist (Eusebius, *Hist. eccl.* 3.39.1 – 9; cf. Acts 21:8 – 9). The Anti-Marcionite Prologue to Mark (possibly as early as c.160–180) speaks of Mark as author and associates him with Peter: "Mark . . . who was called 'stump-fingered' because for the size of the rest of his body he had fingers that were too short. He was Peter's interpreter. After the departure [i.e. death] of Peter, he wrote his Gospel in the regions of Italy." Although this is quite late, the strange remark about Mark's fingers seems unlikely to be invention, so we may still have here real reminiscence.

⁵ Mark 14.31 32.

⁶ "He paints a small picture of himself in the corner of his work" (Theodore Zahn, *Introduction to the New Testament* 2.494 [Edinburgh: 1909]; cf. Vincent Taylor, *The Gospel according to St Mark* [London: Macmillan, 1957] 562; Eugene Boring, Mark [Louisville: Westminster John Knox, 2006] 403, n. 93 [1]). Boring writes powerfully of the "deep shame" of "running away naked" and sees this little narrative as expressing "the final abandonment... one of those who has been called to 'leave everything' to become a disciple of Jesus literally 'leaves everything' to become a nondisciple" (op. cit. 403-404). There is no reason, of course, to divorce such an understanding of the episode from its being Mark's own reminiscence of and shame for the part that he had himself had played in Jesus' story.

## Introduction

In my imaginative reconstruction, however, I venture to go further. Since John Mark's mother lived in Jerusalem, and her home there was large enough to accommodate the Christian community, I imagine her to have been a person of some means, perhaps even one of the "many" women of whom both Luke and Mark speak elsewhere, who accompanied Our Lord during his ministry and supported him and his disciples financially (Mark 15.40-41; Luke 8.1-3). But in any case, the young church as a whole was not large, and she and her son will surely have known these women and listened to their stories. Granted which, I imagine something that the culturally patriarchal traditions of the early church would naturally have tended to overlook or forget, although it seems to me not only possible but even likely—namely, that in composing his account of Jesus, Mark will have drawn not only on what he heard from Peter, but also on his mother's reminiscences and those of her friends.

How then do I imagine these people's story might have developed in the decades following the birth of the church? The church historian Eusebius tells us that as the situation in Jerusalem deteriorated on the eve of the Jewish War of AD 66-70, Christians fled from there to a town called Pella—fleeing, be it noted, *toward* the advancing Roman legions (*Eccles. Hist.* II.5.3). Eusebius connects the actual composition of Mark's gospel, however, with Rome. So perhaps Mary and her family left Jerusalem with the other Christians, but then went on from Pella to Rome?—where possibly Mary already had connections? It is striking, and surely hints at such a possibility, that her son had a Roman name: Mark (Latin, "Marcus").[7] It is equally striking that Mark's gospel shows us Jesus, near the end of his ministry, prophesying the coming Jewish War, and the need to flee from Jerusalem and not turn back (Mark 13.14-20): events so catastrophic for those involved that they are linked with the end of the world.

So I imagine Mark, some years after the death of Peter and shortly after the Jewish War, now living in his mother's house in Rome, where he has completed an early draft of his *Life of Jesus* and tries it out with friends in the Christian community there. Among those friends, I imagine perhaps

---

[7] Throughout Roman history, from the early Republic to the late Empire, "Marcus" is among the most common given names.

Alexander and Rufus: the two sons of Simon of Cyrene whom Mark mentions specifically in his gospel, and in such a way as to suggest that they must have been well-known to the community for whom he wrote (Mark 15.21).

## Mark's Gospel and Performance

How then will Mark have "tried out" his gospel? What will he have seen as its natural setting? In an age before printing, books were generally composed to be read aloud. Indeed, we might say they were composed to be *performed*. As I have long argued—at least since 1993![8] —Mark's text shows clear signs of composition for such a purpose, originally no doubt by a single person trained in the art of rhetorical delivery. Sir Alec McCowen showed us in 1979 that such one-person performance can still be powerful. When I was teaching, I used to show a videotape of McCowen's Mark to my students in New Testament and was always fascinated to see how the text came alive for them as they watched it. I keep hoping that a DVD or Blu-ray Disc will be made of that performance, but it has not happened yet. When I last looked, however, some extracts from it were available on line at YouTube. I commend them heartily. Any actor wanting to perform scripture dramatically could learn from McCowen's handling of the episode of the Gadarene Demoniac, Herod at his court, or Jesus' "if any would come after me" address to the disciples, all of which were among the extracts presented when I last looked.

More recently, Richard Burridge has shown us how dramatically effective Mark's text may be when split up among *three* performers: "Evangelist" , "Jesus" and "everyone else," evidently akin to the three voices that traditionally take their part in liturgical singing of the Passion Narrative. Burridge's Mark is available to watch online (ask your browser for "Richard Burridge rough Mark"), and this, too, I commend heartily.

My own attempt at dramatization could be said, I suppose, to continue along the same trajectory. Influenced over several years by experiences of the

---

[8] See my *Preface to Mark*, especially 167-71.

## Introduction

Passion Narratives on Palm Sunday arranged and directed by David Landon and student members of the Sewanee Theatre Department in All Saints' Chapel at the University of the South, I now imagine the gospel text divided between a group that could be anything from seven—I think that would be the minimum for the kind of thing I envisage—to eleven or even more actors. So not only Jesus, but other figures in the story—Peter, the Syro-Phoenician woman, Caiaphas, the high priest's servant girl, Pilate—can now have their individual voices.

My own contribution to this evolution is that, making use of the imagined "back story" of the text's origin that I have described, for the purposes of performance I now have *two* persons share the role of "evangelist"—one being Mark himself, the other his mother Mary of Jerusalem who, if her role in the early church and in Mark's life was at all as I have imagined it, will clearly have played a significant role in the creation of his gospel. I see her thus representing those faithful women whose voices have surely always echoed in the texts and witness of the Christian church, although their names and specific contributions have fairly consistently been forgotten, overlooked, or denied.

## The Language of Mark's Gospel

Mark wrote in Greek. What kind of Greek? His is the kind of Greek that we call "koine": the common language *(lingua franca)* of the Greeks and virtually everyone else in and around the Mediterranean world from the period following the conquests of Alexander the Great up to and including the Byzantine era. How good was Mark's koine Greek? The answer to that depends to a large extent on what we mean by "good". Clearly, Mark's Greek is not particularly good if we judge it by the standards of classical Greek, or the Asian style affected in some of Paul's later epistles, or the rhetorical elegance of Hebrews, or even the "business" koine of Luke. Indeed, both Matthew and Luke, in making use of what Mark had written, clearly thought that his language needed to be improved and acted upon that thought. But then, as we have said, Greek was the common language of the Mediterranean world at this period. So there were doubtless innumerable versions and argots, all perfectly "good" to those who used and were familiar with them and less "good" to those who were not, just as there are versions and argots of English in the twenty-first century—and probably more so, since the nationwide and international experience of radio, film and television has undoubtedly had the effect of unifying much English usage over the last one hundred or so years.

What then? In a culture where probably less than 15% of people could read, it would be absurd to regard Mark, or anyone who could read and write and actually compose a book, as "uneducated." Indeed, in some respects Mark's literary instincts and understanding are very good—particularly in matters of structure. As a narrative, his, I would argue, is by far the best structured of the four canonical gospels.[9] As for his language: *pace* Matthew and Luke, the fact remains that almost two thousand years after he wrote it, Mark's text continues to be read and valued by millions of by no means ignorant or foolish people. So, bearing in mind George Steiner's observation that, "no stupid literature, art or music lasts,"[10] one must surely conclude that Mark's language, and indeed his text as a whole, are at least as "good" as he needed them to be.

Mark, however, wrote in Greek, and we need to perform his gospel, twenty or so centuries after he wrote it, in English. So what kind of English? There is no definitively correct answer to that question, just as there can never be a definitive for-all-time translation of any text that is in a foreign language and from another culture, though some translations certainly seem to have more staying power than others. McCowen used the Authorized or King James version, which is remarkable for precisely such staying power. It would often amuse me when I showed McCowen's performance to my students to see how the actor's power and integrity swept them past the alleged barrier of language they might normally have spoken of as "too old to communicate in the modern world", with the result that they simply forgot about it! Burridge, by contrast,

---

[9] On Mark's structure, see my *Preface to Mark* 82-125.

[10] George Steiner, *Real Presences* (London: Faber and Faber, 1989) 11.

creates a translation that he calls "rough Mark", in which he deliberately stays as close as possible to the order of Mark's words in Greek. Given all the difficulties involved in working thus from koine Greek, an inflected language where word order may be no more than a tool of emphasis, to modern English, a non-inflected language where word order is normally a crucially important arbiter of meaning, it remains that Burridge's translation is powerful and works well in performance. As you may see—or better, hear—for yourself by listening to it.

But neither of these versions, each masterly in its own way, is in the kind of English that my community speaks. Hence my own little effort is in what, no doubt deriving from Burridge's designation of his translation as "rough Mark," I venture to call "plain Mark." Assuming that Mark wrote in the language of his community, I am trying to render what Lightfoot called "the gospel message of St Mark" in what I consider to be the language of the communities in which I have lived, loved and worked. Whether it works is not, of course, for me to say—although if it doesn't, that will evidently be my fault, not the fault of either Mark or contemporary English.

## The Conclusion to Mark's Gospel

According to all the best manuscripts, Mark's gospel ends at 16.8. The passage that follows 16.8 in our Bibles—that is, Mark 16.9-20—is in a style different from Mark's and is evidently the creation of another and later author, probably writing during the second Christian century. That does not mean that it is to be disdained or ignored, or even that Mark would necessarily have disapproved of it (something we cannot know). It simply means that it is not part of the text that Mark actually wrote. As I tried to show some years ago in my *Preface to Mark* (1993), Mark's structure requires 16.1-8 to have been the intended conclusion.[11] That he wrote further verses that somehow were lost is an idea

---

[11] *Preface to Mark* 120-21.

still posited by a few commentators, but in my view quite mistaken—and to my mind slightly absurd. No "lost ending" ever existed.[12]

In the years since I wrote *Preface to Mark* I have, however, changed my mind regarding the evangelist's intention at 16.8. I now render his closing words *"ephobounto gar,"* translated in RSV, NAB, NRSV and REB as "for they were afraid," by "for they were filled with awe"—more or less as these versions render a similar (though rather stronger) expression, also using Greek *phobeō*, at Mark 4.41, where it describes the male disciples' reaction to Jesus' stilling the storm.[13] I make this change because, as the entire setting together with the immediately previous references to "trembling" and "ecstasy" make clear, the evangelist at 16.8 is not speaking of ordinary fear (fear of the authorities, perhaps), but of what Rudolf Otto in his *Idea of the Holy* taught us to understand as awe and reverence in the presence of the numinous divine, the *"mysterium tremendum et fascinans"* that at once fascinates and terrifies.[14]

The women then proceed, "speaking to no-one on their way"—so I paraphrase Mark's "they said nothing to anyone (*oudeni ouden eipan*)" (16.8). I think my paraphrase brings out what Mark intends us to understand. The

---

[12] See e.g. Boring, *Mark* 451-53: with whose discussion I would only take issue in his suggestion that therefore we should not call Mark 16.9-20 "canonical". On the contrary, though definitely not "Markan", I would argue that "canonical" is precisely what Mark 16.9-20 is, in that the church has chosen to include it in its "canon" of Scripture.

[13] For the purposes of my dramatic rendering of Mark I have treated this element in Mark 4.41 as what it essentially is, that is, a stage direction.

[14] Rudolf Otto, *The Idea of the Holy* (Oxford, 1923), cf. R. H. Lightfoot, *Gospel Message of St Mark* 87-89; Timothy Dwyer, *The Motif of Wonder in the Gospel of Mark* 185-93. The refusal or denigration of such fear is rightly critiqued by Lord Lafeu in Shakespeare's *All's Well that Ends Well*, in a passage that surely applies as much, if not more, to our age as it did to Shakespeare's:
> They say miracles are past; and we have our philosophical persons, to make modern and familiar, things supernatural and causeless. Hence is it that we make trifles of terrors, ensconcing ourselves into seeming knowledge, when we should submit ourselves to an unknown fear.

There is, as I once heard the physicist Arnold Benz point out in a lecture, "nothing at all opposed to the scientific about being in awe at what one has perceived as a scientist."

## Introduction

evangelist is not telling us that the women failed to do what the angel had told them to do. On the contrary, the point is precisely that following that angelic instruction the woman are on a divine mission and have no leisure to stop and exchange greetings or talk until it is completed. We should compare and contrast their behaviour with that of the healed leper earlier in the gospel to whom Jesus says, "Don't talk about this to anyone. Just go! Show yourself to the priest!" (1.44). Instead of doing what Jesus has told him to do, the healed man goes off and at once makes the whole story public—precisely what he has been told *not* to do!

It is true that Mark is somewhat restrained and allusive in his presentation of this part of the story. He can afford be. In the situation in which he will have been presenting it—that is, as we are supposing, the then relatively small community or communities that constituted the Roman church—everyone will have already *known* what the woman did and what had happened afterward: things that we have to infer from elsewhere. I do not doubt that the three women whom Mark identifies as having watched the tomb and visited it on the resurrection morning were identified and named by him precisely because they, and therefore their part in Jesus' story, were known to his community, just as were other people whom he also identifies, such as Alexander and Rufus.[15]

But why is Mark content to be so restrained and allusive? In contrast to Mark the later gospels all affirm quite clearly and unambiguously, each in its own way, that the women did indeed complete their mission. But they also tell us something else. Bluntest is Luke, who affirms that the women told the apostles of the resurrection, and the apostles *did not believe them* (Luke 24.10-11). This surely represents genuinely historical reminiscence, since it is scarcely credible that the church will have *invented* a narrative so unflattering

---

[15] Strikingly, Matthew and Luke, while broadly following Mark, at this point differ. While naming Mary of Magdala, who is common to all three accounts, they offer different names for the women with her. Why? Probably because, out of the small group of women who accompanied Mary of Magdala on that first Easter morning, each evangelist names *the women known to the particular community for which he is writing*. That, as Richard Bauckham has shown us, remains the most likely answer to our question: see Bauckham, *Jesus and the Eyewitnesses: The Gospels as Eyewitness Testimony*, second edition, 48-51.

to the apostles. Yet if true, it requires the women to have completed their mission. The same sequence of events is also implied in John, where Mary of Magdala's joyful "I have seen the Lord" and giving of his message to the disciples is followed immediately ("that same day") by the disciples cowering together "behind locked doors for fear of the Jews", having apparently learned nothing from her message (John 20.18-20). A similar sequence is implicit in Matthew, though more vaguely expressed (28.10-11, 16-17)–and will again be brought out quite explicitly in the mid 2nd century "longer ending" to Mark (Mark 16.9-end). Embarrassment over this apostolic incredulity is, I suspect, most likely the reason for the oblique and indirect quality of Mark's own account of the women's mission.

Thus, while I agree with Eugene Boring that Mark's gospel ends by facing us with a decision[16], against Boring I would respectfully suggest that it is not a decision involving an alleged failure of the women to complete their mission. The decision that faces us is the much more important decision that faced the Eleven: it is whether or not we shall believe the women's word.

## Performing "Dramatic Mark"

In full, Mark's own text takes about two hours to perform. That is about the length of time taken by the McCowen and the Burridge versions.[17] For my part, I determined to limit performance time to something nearer ninety minutes–the average length of a movie or a television drama–so I have made some cuts. The overwhelming majority of these consists in omitting "he said" or "she said" or their equivalent. Such expressions, necessary in a written text or recitation by single person, in performance by a group of actors are merely stage directions or (as one says of liturgical texts) "rubrics": and, as I once heard it put by a great French liturgist whose name I have to my shame forgotten but whose words for some reason remain etched in my memory, "On

---

[16] Eugene Boring, *Mark* 449.

[17] In *Preface to Mark* I see that I suggested "seventy minutes". I was being wildly optimistic.

ne récit pas une rubrique, on l'exécute!" By the same token, since there are to be actors, I have also turned various places where Mark, with only one story teller, merely *implies* speech or dialogue, into direct speech that the actors can perform (e.g. Mark 9.2-7, 15.44-45). I have also made four brief cuts (namely Mark 4.10-20, 9.43-49, 10.10-12, and 13.19-20) whose omission, I hope, does not detract from the overall message of his gospel.

Whom, then, do I have in mind as possible readers and performers for my "dramatic Mark"? Most evidently, I hope that it will work and be useful for amateur groups who simply enjoy performance and interpretation, either performing for their own communities or congregations, or else just reading together for the pleasure and enlightenment that performing any text with friends can give—in other words, just such a group as performed an earlier draft of this text in Exeter Cathedral in 2024. That, however, is not to say that I don't believe that *Dramatic Mark* has possibilities beyond that. Quite the contrary. Our Exeter group treated it pretty well as "sound-radio drama" in their 2024 production. But my experience (to which I have already referred) of portions of the gospel narratives being presented by young actors from the Sewanee Theatre Department during the early 2000s convinces me that it could certainly also be performed more elaborately as live theatre. It could also be used as the basis for a film or television script, with the two voices of the Evangelist, following the Prelude, as voice-over. All would depend on the time, talents and resources available.

As a final word, I should perhaps confess to some irritation with the person (well-meaning no doubt) who asked me what "right" I thought I had to "do" all this to a canonical text. My (certainly defensive!) reply is that I haven't "done" anything to a canonical text. Canonical Mark remains what it is, available to all in the pages of the New Testament. It will, I trust, remain so long after this little effort of mine is lost and forgotten. I regard myself merely as someone trying to make Mark's gospel message, as best I can understand it, communicate in my particular time and my particular situation. I have done what I can to achieve that.

**Christopher Bryan**
Monday in Holy Week, 2024

# Dramatic Mark

### Cast in order of appearance:

Mary of Jerusalem, John Mark's mother (in her late-sixties), who during the rehearsal will play Evangelist 2
John Mark, author of the gospel (in his early fifties), who during the rehearsal will play Evangelist 1
Apphia
Alexander
Rufus
Other friends of Mary and Mark
These, during the rehearsal, will play:
Jesus
John the Baptizer, God, Peter, other disciples, synagogue members, scribes, Pharisees, bystanders, lepers, parents of sick children, woman with Haemorrhages, members of the crowd, the High Priest, Pontius Pilate, aide to Pilate, soldiers, centurion, angel at the tomb *et cetera*.

*Dramatic Mark* was first performed at the Cathedral Church of Saint Peter in Exeter on the 18th of May 2024 by the Cathedral Players under the direction of the Reverend Canon David Gunn-Johnson, Priest Vicar, with the following cast:

**Mary of Jerusalem, Mark's mother / afterwards Evangelist 2:** Susan Gunn-Johnson
**John Mark / afterwards Evangelist 1:** James Cotter
**Apphia:** Frances Manhire
**Jesus:** Nigel Mason
**John the Baptizer, God, Peter, other disciples, synagogue members, scribes, Pharisees, bystanders, lepers, parents of sick children, woman with Haemorrhages, members of the crowd, soldiers, optio, centurion, angel et cetera:** Clare Bryden, Christopher Hampton, Rachel Hiland, Frances Manhire, and Jeremy Rawlings.

**Guitarist:** Brian Lawless
**Percussion:** David Gunn-Johnson

Before and during production, David Gunn-Johnson worked closely with me on preparation of the first draft of the text, and the result owed much to his wisdom. Most notably, I wrote the Prelude, which I believe works well in introducing 21st century audiences to what is going on, entirely at David's suggestion. My dramatization of Mark's passion narrative draws heavily, with his permission, on a version created some years ago by David Landon for use at All Saints' Chapel, Sewanee, whilst my dramatization of the whole gospel owes much to ideas exchanged and inspiration gained over several years with him and groups of seminarians at the University of the South in our *Drama of the Word* seminars. And as often in the past, my final text owes much to the careful eye of the Reverend Vicki Burgess. Such processes are, indeed, clear examples of the fact that authorship is seldom, is ever, a solitary exercise.

# Prelude

**Scene:** *Rome, circa 71 AD. A reception room in the house of John Mark's mother Mary.*

*Enter Mary, who looks around her, then calls.*

| | |
|---|---|
| **Mary:** | Mark? Mark! Are you ready? |
| **Mark:** | *(offstage):* Just making a little change, mother! Won't be long! |
| **Mary:** | Well you can't go on making changes all night. They'll be here any minute. |

*Enter Mark, carrying a couple of scripts, one of which he gives to his mother.*

| | |
|---|---|
| **Mark:** | Here we are! All done! I know I'm fussing, but I've got to try and get this right. It isn't just a life of any great man we're writing. It's the story of Jesus, the greatest story ever told! |
| **Mary:** | Yes, dear, I know. I was there. |
| **Mark:** | I know you were, mother. And I was just a kid who didn't see any of it! Everyone insists on calling me Peter's 'interpreter' but we both know half my stuff's what you and your friends have told me. I sometimes think you women remember what happened better than Peter did. |
| **Mary:** | We probably do. Peter wasn't paying the bills. There's nothing like a dash of accountancy for focusing the mind. But you *did* see one bit of it. |
| **Mark:** | Yes, well, I think we'll maybe cut that bit out. It's embarrassing. |

**Mary:** We dam' well won't! You were hardly more than a boy, it was the middle of the night and you were supposed to be in bed asleep! And then you frighten us all out of our wits running in out of the dark, stark naked and scared stiff! There's no way you're leaving that out.

**Mark:** Just kidding, mother. It's still in—even the bit about me being starkers. It'll be my own little signature. *(He pauses, then, more seriously)* In a way, I can't help thinking it's all our signatures. I mean—that night—everyone just ran. We abandoned him. And when we did that we left behind us everything that mattered. We *all* fled naked. I think that's why I have to tell his story. I must tell it.

**Mary.** Yes dear, I think you must. And you will.

*Apphia appears, followed by Alexander and Rufus, all carrying scripts. Several others follow them as Mary speaks.*

**Mary:** Here's Apphia! And Alexander and Rufus! And all of you! Come in, come in!

**Mark:** Great! We're here. You all ready to go?

**Apphia.** We think so.

**Alexander:** This is just a practice, isn't it?

**Rufus:** It'd better be! I didn't get a chance to look at it 'til this morning.

**Mark:** Of course it is.

*Gentle music—strings: a violin or a guitar.*

*They all take their positions, and the first reading of the first draft of Mark's narrative begins.*

# Prologue

## Witness to the Coming One (Mark 1.1-8)

**Mark:** *henceforth* **Evangelist 1:** The beginning of the good news of Jesus the Messiah, the Anointed One, Son of God!

**Mary,** *henceforth* **Evangelist 2:** As it is written in the prophet Isaiah—

> Behold, I send my messenger ahead of you,
> who will prepare your way:
> The voice of one crying out in the wilderness:
> Prepare the way of the Lord!
> Make his paths straight!

— even so, John the baptizer appeared in the wilderness. He came with a proclamation—

| | |
|---|---|
| **John Baptist:** | Be baptized! Turn back to God, who will forgive your sins! |
| **Evangelist 1:** | Huge crowds from the Judean countryside and Jerusalem were flocking to him and being baptised in the River Jordan, confessing to their sins. |
| **Evangelist 2:** | Now John was dressed in rough camel hair with a leather belt, and he ate locusts and wild honey. He spoke like a herald. |
| **John Baptist:** | After me Someone is coming who is far, far greater than I. I'm not fit to kneel and untie his sandals. I baptize you with water, but he will baptize you with the Holy Spirit! |
| | *Drumbeat* |

# Act I

The Ministry of Jesus:
in and around Galilee

(Mark 1.9-8.21)

**Evangelist 2:** In those days Jesus came from Nazareth of Galilee and was baptized by John in Jordan. As Jesus was coming up out of the water he saw the heavens torn open and the Spirit descending on him like a dove! And there was a voice from heaven.

**God:** You are my Son, my beloved. In you I have great joy!

*Chime.*

**Evangelist 1:** At once the Spirit thrusts him out into the wilderness. And he was in the wilderness forty days, tested by Satan. The wild animals were his friends,[18] and the angels served him.

*Chime.*

**Evangelist 2:** Now after John was arrested, Jesus came into Galilee proclaiming the good news of God:

---

[18] I here paraphrase Mark so as to bring out what I believe was his intention. His expression "wild beasts were with him" (NRSV Mark 1.13) ("with" here rendering μετὰ plus the genitive) implies companionship and association, not hostility or threat. Following the "testing" by Satan, in which Jesus (whom Paul called "the second Adam') is by implication successful, Mark sees him regaining the position which was Adam's before the fall, with the beasts as his companions and playfellows, and the angels as his servants. Indeed, Newman's hymn has it more or less exactly right:

> O loving wisdom of our God!
> When all was sin and shame,
> a second Adam to the fight
> and to the rescue came.
> O wisest love! that flesh and blood,
> which did in Adam fail,
> should strive afresh against the foe,
> should strive and should prevail.

I am aware that this interpretation is disputed, but personally I find it hard to suppose that anyone familiar with interpretative traditions surrounding Genesis 1-3 such as those in the *Life of Adam* and the *Apocalypse of Moses* (both clearly popular and simple in style) could avoid hearing echoes of them in Mark's narrative. See further my *Preface to Mark* 141-43; Eugene Boring, *Mark* 48; and BDAG μετὰ A.1 and 2.

## Act I – The Ministry of Jesus: in and around Galilee

**Jesus:** The time is fulfilled! God's kingdom is near! Turn back to God! Trust the good news!

**Evangelist 2:** As Jesus passed along the Sea of Galilee, he saw Simon and his brother Andrew casting a net into the sea, for they were fishermen.

**Jesus:** Follow me, and I'll show you how to fish for people!

**Evangelist 2:** Immediately they left their nets and followed him. As he went on he saw James son of Zebedee and his brother John. They were in their boat mending nets. And there and then he called them.

**Jesus:** Follow me!

**Evangelist 2:** And they left their father Zebedee in the boat with the hired men and followed him.

*Drumbeat*

**Evangelist 1:** They come to Capernaum. Straight away on the Sabbath he entered the synagogue and was teaching. They were astounded at his teaching.

**Synagogue member:** He talks with such authority!

**Another Synagogue member:** But not at all like the scribes!

**Evangelist 2:** Now there was a man in the synagogue with an unclean spirit. And he shrieked—

**Man with unclean spirit** *(different demonic voices in crescendo):*

What do you want with us, Jesus of Nazareth?

Leave us alone!

| | |
|---|---|
| | Have you come to destroy us? |
| | I know you, who you are! THE HOLY ONE OF GOD! |
| **Jesus:** | *(powerfully though not necessarily loudly: cutting across the demonic cry with an authority that brooks no denial)* Silence! Come out of him! |
| **Evangelist 1:** | The unclean spirit tore the man and screamed—and came out of him. Everyone was totally stunned! |
| **Bystanders** | *(different voices)* |
| | What is this? |
| | A new teaching! |
| | With authority! |
| | He orders demons about! |
| | And they do what he tells them! |
| **Evangelist 1:** | Jesus' fame began to spread through all the surrounding districts of Galilee. |
| | *Drumbeat.* |
| **Evangelist 1:** | On leaving synagogue they went straight to Simon and Andrew's house. James and John went with them. |
| **John:** | *(quietly and discreetly, to Jesus)* It's Simon's mother-in-law, teacher. She's in bed with a fever. |
| **Peter:** | *(similarly discreet)* Teacher, she's really sick. None of us knows what to do.[19] |

---

[19] Thus (see the Introduction, 18-19) I try to render in direct speech what is implicit in Mark's "And straightway they tell him of her" (Mark 1.30). As for the actual sentiment—we should perhaps recall that even as late as the time of Jane Austen (see *Sense and Sensibility* Vol. III, Chapt. vii), before the discovery of things like aspirin, even with the best care available a bout of fever could be fatal.

## Act I – The Ministry of Jesus: in and around Galilee

**Evangelist 2:** Wasting no time Jesus came. He took her by the hand and raised her up – and the fever left her! And she began to serve them.

*Chime.*

**Evangelist 1:** That evening at sunset they kept bringing to him anyone who was sick or possessed. The whole city was gathered at the door. And he cured many sick and drove out many demons.

**Evangelist 2:** He wouldn't allow the demons to speak, because they knew who he was.

*Drumbeat*

**Evangelist 1:** In the morning, while it was still dark, he got up and went out to a deserted place. And there he prayed.

*A pause*

**Evangelist 2:** But Simon and his companions hunted him down.

**Disciples:** *(different voices)*

Jesus!

Jesus!

There he is!

There you are!

**Peter:** Everyone's looking for you!

**Jesus:** *(patiently, but already a tad wearily)* Let's go to the other market towns so I can proclaim the message there as well. That's what I've come out to do.

**Evangelist 1:** And he went throughout all Galilee, proclaiming the message in their synagogues and casting out demons.

*Drumbeat.*

| | |
|---|---|
| **Evangelist 2:** | A leper came to him, pleading with him. |
| **Leper:** | Teacher, I beg you! If you're willing, you can make me clean. |
| **Evangelist 2:** | Jesus was moved to indignation. He stretched out his hand and touched him. |
| **Jesus:** | *(gently)* I am willing. Be made clean! |
| **Evangelist 1:** | The leprosy left him immediately, and he was clean. |
| **Jesus:** | Don't talk about this to anyone. Just go! Show yourself to the priest. And make the offering Moses commanded as witness to them. |
| **Evangelist 1:** | But the man he'd cured went out and started telling everyone, spreading the story far and wide! |
| **Evangelist 2:** | So Jesus couldn't any longer go into a town—not openly. He stayed in remote places. Yet people kept coming to him! |
| | *Drumbeat.* |
| **Evangelist 1** | When he returned to Capernaum after some days, it was reported— |
| **Bystanders** | *(several voices, murmuring):* |
| | He's at home! |
| | There's a huge crowd there! No room for anyone! |
| | Not even in front of the door! |
| | *(awestruck)* He's speaking God's word to us! |
| **Evangelist 2:** | Then some folk came bringing a paralyzed man. When they couldn't get him to Jesus because of the crowd, they removed the roof above him! They dug through it, |

| | |
|---|---|
| | then let down the mat with the paralytic on it. Jesus saw their faith – and spoke to the paralysed man. |
| **Jesus:** | Child, your sins are forgiven. |
| **Evangelist 2:** | Now some of the scribes were sitting there, and they had questions. |
| **Scribes** | *(several voices):* |
| | Why does the fellow talk like this? |
| | It's blasphemy! |
| | Who can forgive sins but God? |
| **Evangelist 2:** | Jesus sees at once what they're thinking. |
| **Jesus:** | Why are you asking such questions? Tell me which is easier? – to say to a paralysed man, 'Your sins are forgiven,' or to say, 'Stand up! Take your mat and walk'? But that you may know that the Son of Man has authority on earth to forgive sins – *(he turns to the man who has been paralysed)* – you, friend, I'm talking to you! Stand up, take your mat, and go home! |
| **Evangelist 2:** | And the man who'd been paralysed stood up and immediately took the mat and went out – with everybody watching! |
| **Bystanders** | *(several voices, amazed):* |
| | I can't believe it! |
| | Glory to God! |
| | Praise the Lord! |
| | We've never seen anything like this! |
| | *Chime.* |

| | |
|---|---|
| **Evangelist 1:** | Jesus went out again beside the sea. A whole crowd gathered round him, and he taught them. As he was walking along he saw Levi son of Alphaeus sitting at the tax office. |
| **Jesus:** | Levi, son of Alphaeus—yes, you! Follow me! |
| **Evangelist 1:** | And he got up and followed him. And Jesus dined at his house. Many tax collectors and sinners were dining there too, with Jesus and his disciples, for there were many of them following him. The Pharisees' scribes saw it. |
| **Scribe:** | He's eating with sinners and tax collectors! |
| **Another Scribe:** | Eating and *drinking* with them! |
| **Jesus:** | Those who are well don't need the doctor, do they? But those who are sick do! I haven't come to call the righteous, but sinners. |
| | *Chime* |
| **Evangelist 1:** | Now John's disciples and the Pharisees used to keep the usual fast days. So people come to Jesus and ask him. |
| **People** | *(several voices):* |
| | Why do John's disciples keep the fasts? |
| | And the Pharisees' disciples keep them! |
| | But your disciples don't! |
| **Jesus:** | Wedding guests can't fast while the bridegroom is with them, can they? As long as they have the bridegroom with them, they can't fast. But there'll come a time when the bridegroom is taken away from them, and then they will fast! No one sews a piece of unshrunk cloth on an old |

Act I – The Ministry of Jesus: in and around Galilee

        cloak; otherwise, the patch pulls away from it, the new from the old, and a worse tear is made. And no one puts new wine into old wineskins; otherwise, the wine bursts the skins, and the wine is lost and so are the skins. But new wine is put into fresh skins.

*Drumbeat*

**Evangelist 2:** One Sabbath he was going through the grain fields, and as they went his disciples began to pluck heads of grain. The Pharisees objected.

**Pharisee:** Why do your disciples do what isn't lawful on the Sabbath?

**Jesus:** *(slightly amused?)* Have you never read what David did? When he and his men were hungry and needed food? How he entered the house of God when Abiathar was high priest and ate the bread of the Presence— which isn't lawful for anyone to eat except the priests? And he gave some to his men! The Sabbath was made for people, not people for the Sabbath. So the Son of Man is lord even of the Sabbath.

*Drumbeat.*

**Evangelist 1:** Again he went to synagogue and a man was there who had a withered hand. And some were watching him.

**Scribes:** *(two voices, sotto voce)* Will he cure on the sabbath?

If he does, he's breaking the law. We bring charges.

*(enthusiastically)* Yes!

**Jesus:** *(gently)* Stand up. Come out here, where we can see you! *(he turns to the scribes)* Now – you who are so busy watching me – tell me! Is it lawful on the Sabbath to do good or to do harm? To save life or to kill?

**Jesus:** *(sad and angry)* You people—your hearts are stone. *(to the man with the withered hand, gently)* Friend, stretch out your hand!

**Evangelist 1:** He stretched it out—and his hand was completely restored!

*Chime*

**Evangelist 1:** The Pharisees went out and immediately conspired with the Herodians[20] against him, how to destroy him.

*Rattle*

**Evangelist 2:** Jesus withdrew with his disciples to the sea. And a huge crowd followed! From Galilee and Judea and Jerusalem. From Idumea and Transjordan. And round Tyre and Sidon. A huge crowd! They heard what he was doing and came to him.

**Evangelist 1:** He told his disciples to have a boat ready for him because of the crowd, so they wouldn't crush him. For he had cured many, so that all the sick were crowding in on him to touch him. Whenever the unclean spirits saw him, they fell down before him, crying out.

**Unclean Spirits** *(several voices):*

You're the Son!

Son of God!

---

[20] As commentators invariably point out, this is a strange alliance, for in many respects the two groups are quite opposed to one another. They have in common, however, a dislike of what Jesus represents. The Pharisees, influential with the people but lacking political power, and the Herodians, not especially popular but influential with (as we say) "the people who matter" can help each other. So they cooperate.

## Act I – The Ministry of Jesus: in and around Galilee)

| | |
|---|---|
| **Jesus:** | *(sternly commanding)* Do not speak of me. Do not make me known. |
| | *Drumbeat* |
| **Evangelist 2:** | He went up the mountain and called to him those whom he wanted, and they came to him. |
| **Jesus:** | I am appointing you, twelve of you. You are to be with me, and I will send you out. I give you authority to proclaim the kingdom, and to cast out demons. |
| **Evangelist:** | There was Simon. |
| **Jesus:** | I'm going to call you "Peter" – |
| **Evangelist 2:** | – that is "Rock."[21] |
| **Evangelist 1:** | And James son of Zebedee, and John, James's brother. |
| **Jesus:** | *(chuckling)* I'm naming you two "Boanerges." |
| **Evangelist 2:** | That is "Sons of Thunder"![22] |
| **Evangelist 1:** | And Andrew and Philip. |
| **Evangelist 2:** | And Bartholomew and Matthew and Thomas. |
| **Evangelist 1:** | And James son of Alphaeus, and Thaddaeus. |
| **Evangelist 2:** | And Simon the Cananaean. |

---

[21] "Peter" at Mark 3.16, is not just a nickname, "Rocky." It implies a foundation and a pillar (cf. Matt. 16.18, Gal 2.9). It echoes Abram being renamed Abraham (Gen. 12.1, 17.5), who in reference to his role as the first Israelite is likewise called "the rock" (Isa. 51.1-2). Peter will be so addressed throughout the narrative, until his falling asleep in Gethsemane when he has been told to "watch" shows him so very un-rock-like (Mark 14.37).

[22] For the purposes of the drama I have treated "Sons of Thunder" as a humorous reference to a personality trait (cf. Mark 9.38, Luke 9.54): but this is by no means certain. In fact we have no certain explanation of either "Boanerges" or "Sons of Thunder". Neither, apparently, had Matthew or Luke, both of whom omit the expressions in their own lists of the twelve (Matt. 10.2-3, Luke 6.14). In contrast to the regular use of "Peter", neither James nor John are referred to by their new names again, either by the evangelist or by anyone else.

| | |
|---|---|
| **Evangelist 1:** | And Judas Iscariot. |
| **Evangelist 2:** | The one who betrayed him. |
| | *Rattle* |
| **Evangelist 1:** | Then he went home. And again there was such a crowd gathered, they couldn't even eat. |
| **Evangelist 2:** | When his family heard about it they went out to restrain him.[23] |
| **Jesus' family** | *(various voices of Jesus elder brothers and sisters)* |
| | Someone needs to take charge of him. |
| | He's beside himself. |
| | He's completely lost his mind. |
| **Evangelist 1:** | But the scribes – down from Jerusalem – they were saying, |
| **Scribes** | *(various somewhat clerical voices):* |
| | He is possessed – by Beelzebul! |
| | It is by the prince of demons that he drives out demons![24] |
| **Evangelist 1:** | Jesus confronted them. |

---

[23] The references to Jesus' family in the episodes described here (Mark 3.21, 31-32) and at Mark 6.1-6 (see also note 29 below) are most naturally understood as indicating that Joseph was now dead. It is inconceivable that the head of the household would not have been mentioned if still around. Moreover, the view of Jesus' brothers that they have a right, and even perhaps a duty, to take charge of Jesus surely implies that they are senior to him in the family hierarchy: which is to say, they are his elders. The oldest brother would of course, at his father's death, have become head of the household: senior to Jesus and to his mother Mary. All of which leads me to accept the view generally associated with the late fourth century bishop Epiphanius of Salamis: that Jesus' "brothers" and "sisters" referred to at Mark 3.31-32 and 6.3 are Joseph's children by a previous marriage.

[24] As Mark presents them, the objections of Jesus' family members are largely personal and without real substance. The scribes' objections, in that they are in some sense theological, are altogether more sinister. We may see in them the seeds of the charge of blasphemy that will eventually be brought against Jesus by the Sanhedrin.

## Act I – The Ministry of Jesus: in and around Galilee

**Jesus:** So tell me, just exactly *how* does Satan drive out Satan? If a kingdom's divided against itself, that kingdom can't stand, can it? And if a house is divided against itself, that house won't be able to stand, will it? And if Satan's risen up against himself and is divided, *he* cannot stand. He's finished! No one can enter a strong man's house and plunder his property without first tying up the strong man. Then the house can be plundered. *(Pauses, then very deliberately).* Truly, I tell you, people will be forgiven for their sins and all sorts of blasphemies. But those who keep on slandering the Holy Spirit are making themselves incapable of receiving forgiveness. And the results of that are eternal.

**Evangelist 1:** He said this, because they kept on saying he was possessed by an unclean spirit.[25]

*Drumbeat*

**Evangelist 2:** Then his mother and his brothers arrived. Staying

---

[25] I paraphrase somewhat in an effort to bring out what I think is the meaning of a saying that has caused many good people anguish. Undoubtedly C. E. B. Cranfield was correct in saying "with absolute confidence to anyone who is overwhelmed by fear that they have committed this sin, that the fact that they are so troubled is itself sure proof that they have not committed it" (*Gospel According to Mark* 142). The slander against the Holy Spirit of which Our Lord speaks appears to consist in this: that when Jesus offers the divine healing and forgiveness, the scribes repeatedly declare such forgiveness and healing to be the work of an unclean spirit—I say "repeatedly" advisedly: note the use of the imperfect tense ἔλεγον at 3.30, which I have rendered by "kept on saying". Such an insistence, so long as it is maintained, renders them incapable of being forgiven because it constitutes a *refusal* of the divine healing and forgiveness, and even God cannot (or, at least, will not) give us what we refuse to accept. Hence Miss Foot–the somewhat comical character in Sally Vickers's *Dancing Backwards*–is entirely correct: "That is the true sin against the Holy Ghost–the refusal of grace and mercy" (Ch. 26). She is also, incidentally, right in what she says next, namely, that "intensity is not an index of spiritual depth." So to this day there are many who are willing condemn others, even daring as they do so to invoke with passion the name and person of Jesus. It does not follow that they are right, or that their act of condemnation is also Jesus' act of condemnation.

| | outside, they sent and asked him to come out to them. Now there was a crowd sitting round him. |
|---|---|
| **Crowd** | *(various voices):* |
| | It's your mother and your brothers and sisters! |
| | They're outside, asking for you. |
| **Jesus:** | Who is my mother? Who are my brothers and sisters? I look at all of you—and it's you! You who are listening to me! Here is my mother! And my brothers! And my sisters! Whoever does God's will is my brother and sister and mother. |
| | *Drumbeat* |
| **Evangelist 2:** | Again he began to teach beside the sea. A very large crowd gathered round him, so he got into a boat and sat in it; and the whole crowd was beside the sea on the land. He taught them in parables. |
| **Jesus: Listen!** | A sower went out to sow. And as he sowed, some seed fell along the path, and the birds came and devoured it. Other seed fell on rocky ground, where it had little soil. When the sun rose it was scorched, and since it had no root it withered away. Other seed fell among thorns and the thorns grew up and choked it. And it yielded no grain. And other seed fell into good soil and brought forth grain, growing up and increasing and yielding thirtyfold and sixtyfold and a hundredfold. Who has ears to hear, let them hear. |
| **Evangelist 2:** | When he was alone, those who were following him, along with the twelve, would ask him. |
| **Disciple:** | Tell us about your parables, teacher. |

## Act I – The Ministry of Jesus: in and around Galilee

**Another Disciple:** What did that last one mean?

**Jesus:** To you has been given the secret of God's kingdom. For those outside everything is in parables. So they see but do not perceive, they hear but do not understand; lest they should turn again and be forgiven.

*Drumbeat*

**Jesus:** Don't you understand this parable? How then will you understand all the parables? Do you bring in a lamp so as to put it under a bowl or under the bed? Of course not! You put it on a lampstand! Nothing is hidden, except to be made manifest. Nor is anything secret, except to come to light. If you've ears to hear, then hear!

*Drumbeat*

**Jesus:** Listen carefully! The measure you give will be the measure you get, and still more will be given you. For to those who have, more will be given; and from those who don't have, even what they do have will be taken away.

*Drumbeat*

The kingdom of God is like this. You scatter seed on the ground. You go to bed at night and get up in the morning, and meanwhile the seed sprouts and grows— you have no idea how! The earth produces a crop by itself: first the blade, then the ear, then the full grain. But as soon as the grain is ripe, you put in the sickle, because harvest has come.

*Drumbeat*

How shall we picture God's kingdom? Or what parable shall we use for it? It's like a mustard seed. When it's

|  |  |
|---|---|
|  | sown on the ground, it is smallest of all the seeds. Yet once it's been sown it springs up and grows to be the greatest of all shrubs and puts forth large branches so that the birds of the air can make nests in its shade. |
| **Evangelist 1:** | With many such parables he would speak the word to them, so far as they were able to hear it. He never spoke to the people except in parables. But privately to his disciples he explained everything. |
|  | *Drumbeat* |
| **Jesus:** | *(tired)* It's evening. Let's cross to the other side of the lake. |
| **Evangelist 2:** | And leaving the crowd, they took him with them in the boat, just as he was. And other boats were with him. *(beginning sounds of rain and wind)* Soon a great storm of wind arose. *(sounds of storm, rain, thunder, and crashing waves).* |
| **Disciples** | *(various voices, shouting over storm):* |
|  | The waves are coming over the bow! |
|  | We're being swamped. |
|  | Where's Jesus? |
|  | He's in the stern! |
|  | *(exasperated)* He's asleep! On a cushion! |
|  | *(rising panic)* Teacher! Teacher, we're sinking! |
|  | Don't you care?! |
| **Evangelist 1:** | Jesus awoke. |
| **Jesus:** | *(rebuking the wind and addressing the sea)* Winds, be silent! Waters, be still! |

## Act I – The Ministry of Jesus: in and around Galilee

*(Storm noises die away: there is a calm)*

*(chime)*

**Jesus:** Why are you afraid? Have you no faith?

**Disciples:** *(sotto voce, to each other, two or three voices, awestruck):*

Who is this?

Even the wind and the sea obey him!

*Chime.*

**Evangelist 1:** They came to the other side of the lake, to the country of the Gerasenes. And when he had come out of the boat, there met him a man with an unclean spirit, who lived among the tombs. And no one could bind him, not even with a chain. He'd been bound often with fetters and chains, but the chains he wrenched apart, and the fetters he broke in pieces. No one was strong enough to overpower him. Night and day among the tombs and on the mountains he was crying out and bruising himself. When he saw Jesus at a distance, he ran up and flung himself down before him.

**Demons** *(shrieking and in pain: plural voices in semi-unison).* What do you want with me, Jesus? Son of the Most High God, what do you want?

**Jesus:** *(calm but firm)* Out, unclean spirit! Come out of him!

**Demons:** *(still shrieking, tormented)* In God's name don't torment me!

**Jesus:** *(gently but with authority)* What is your name?

**Demons:** *(still shrieking)* My name is Legion! Legion!! For we are many!

|   |   |
|---|---|
|   | Don't cast us out, Jesus! Don't cast us out! |
|   | Look at the pigs! Up on the hill! Lots of pigs! Gobbling! |
|   | Nasty pigs! Unclean! Send us into them, son of God! Send us! |
| **Jesus:** | *(wearily)* If you must. |
| **Evangelist 2:** | And the unclean spirits came out and entered the pigs. And the entire herd—there were about two thousands of them! — plunged down the steep bank into the sea and were drowned. |
| **Evangelist 2:** | The herdsmen fled. They told their news in the town and the countryside, and people came out to see what had happened. They come to Jesus, and they see the demoniac sitting there, clothed and in his right mind—the man who had had the Legion. And they were afraid. |
| **People** | *(several voices):* We saw it all! |
|   | He cured the crazy man. |
|   | But then the pigs went crazy! |
|   | Please sir, just leave us alone! |
|   | You're a scary man. |
|   | You need to go.[26] |
| **Evangelist 1:** | But then, as he was getting into the boat, there was the man who'd been possessed! |
| **Man:** | Lord, master, take me with you. |
| **Jesus:** | *(gently)* No, friend, you should go home. Tell your own people what the God of Israel in his mercy has done for you. |

---

[26] Something like the preceding direct conversations is implied by Mark 5.10-13, 15-18.

## Act I – The Ministry of Jesus: in and around Galilee

**Evangelist 1:** So the man went off and started proclaiming throughout Decapolis what Jesus had done for him.

*Drumbeat*

**Evangelist 2:** When Jesus had crossed again in the boat to the other side, a great crowd gathered. He was at the lakeside.

**Evangelist 1:** And along comes a man called Jairus, a leader of one of the synagogues. When he sees Jesus he throws himself at his feet.

**Jairus:** Teacher, my little daughter's dying! I beg you! Come and lay your hands on her. So she may be healed and live!

**Jesus:** I will come.

**Evangelist 1:** A huge crowd followed and thronged about him.

**Evangelist 2:** Now there was a woman who had suffered from haemorrhages for twelve years. She'd suffered much under many physicians and spent all that she had. Yet she was no better, but rather worse. She'd heard the reports about Jesus.

**The Woman:** *(sotto voce: talking to herself)* If I can just touch his cloak, I'll get well.

**Evangelist 1:** So she came up behind him in the crowd and touched his cloak. And straight away the blood dried up.

**The Woman:** *(still sotto voce)* It's better. I'm cured! I can feel it!

**Evangelist 2:** Jesus knew at once that power had gone out of him. He span round in the crowd—

**Jesus:** Who touched my cloak?

**Disciples** *(at least two voices):* Teacher, what are you saying?

|  |  |
|---|---|
|  | You're in the middle of a crowd!<br>How can you ask, 'Who touched me?'! |
| **Evangelist 2:** | —but Jesus went on looking round to see who it was. The woman—terrified and trembling, [for she'd been ritually unclean and should not have presumed to touch the teacher, and yet she knew she'd received a miracle[27]]—she came and fell at his feet. |
| **The Woman:** | It was me teacher. I've been so sick. I knew if I could just touch your cloak I'd be better! *And I am!* But I shouldn't have done it. I'm unclean! I've defiled you. O sir, please, please forgive me![28] |
| **Jesus:** | *(gently)* Daughter! Daughter! Your faith has saved you. Go in peace. You are free from your affliction. |
|  | *Chime* |
| **Bystander:** | Master, look, while you were talking — here are people come from the synagogue-leader's house. |
| **Person from the house:** | I'm very sorry Jairus. Your daughter has died. |
| **2nd Person from the house:** | Why trouble the Teacher further? |
| **Jesus:** | Don't be afraid, Jairus. Have faith. |
| **Evangelist 2:** | He let no one to go with him except Peter and James and James' brother John. They come into the leader's house, *(sounds of weeping and mourning)* and he sees a tumult. |

---

[27] These words are not in Mark's text, and in production could be omitted. But it is may be helpful for a 21st century audience to be given reasons for the woman's fear: reasons which Mark could reasonably have expected his original audience to understand without his spelling them out.

[28] Not in Mark's text, but something like it is required if we are to turn the evangelist's indirect—"and confessed the whole truth" (5.33c)—into direct speech for an actor.

## Act I – The Ministry of Jesus: in and around Galilee

| | |
|---|---|
| **Jesus:** | Why are you wailing and weeping? The child isn't dead. She is asleep. |
| **A mourner:** | For God's sake, man! That's fools' talk. |
| **Another mourner:** | The child's gone. |
| **Jesus:** | Out of the house, all of you! Jairus, fetch your wife. Peter, James, John—you too. Come with us! |
| **Evangelist 2:** | So they went in to the child. Jesus took her by the hand. |
| **Jairus' wife:** | *(softly: to her husband)* Look! Her lashes are fluttering! Her eyes are opening! She's waking![29] |
| **Jesus:** | *(also softly)* Talitha cum! Get up, lass! |
| **Evangelist 2:** | And straight away the girl got up and walked about. She was twelve years old. |
| **Jairus:** | Can I believe what I'm seeing? God of Israel, he has brought her back! |
| **Jairus' wife:** | Teacher, how can we ever thank you? |
| **Jesus:** | Don't let anyone know about this. And *(slightly amused)* give her something to eat! |
| | *Chime.* |
| **Evangelist 1:** | He went away from there. He comes to his home town, and his disciples are following along. When sabbath came he began to teach in the synagogue. And many who heard him were astonished. |

---

[29] Again, I have here turned into direct speech what is surely implied by Mark 5.39-43. In particular, I've given Jairus and his wife lines in an attempt to reflect Mark's very emphatic "καὶ ἐξέστησαν εὐθὺς ἐκστάσει μεγάλῃ" –literally, "And they were straightway astounded with a great, utter amazement."

| | |
|---|---|
| **Townsfolk** | *(different voices):* Where did this man get all this? |
| | All this wisdom! |
| | What about these mighty works he does? |
| | Isn't he supposed to be a carpenter? |
| | He's Mary's son, isn't he? |
| | And James and Joses, and Judas and Simon—aren't they his brothers? |
| | And aren't his sisters here with us?[30] |
| | I don't trust him!![31] |
| **Jesus:** | A prophet is never without honour, except in his home town among his own people and in his own house. |
| **Evangelist 1:** | And he could do no mighty work there—except he laid his hands on a few sick people and healed them. For the rest – |
| **Jesus:** | *(wearily)* I marvel at their unbelief. |
| | *Drumbeat.* |
| **Evangelist 2:** | He was going about among nearby villages, teaching. |

---

[30] If the siblings of Jesus referred to here and at 3.31, 31.35 are all the deceased Joseph's children by an earlier marriage (see note 23 above) the description of Jesus as "Mary's son," while in itself a normal way of speaking of someone whose father was dead but whose mother was still living, will inevitably also have indicated a *difference* between Jesus and Mary on the one hand, and the rest of the family on the other: and this difference may have been one factor in tension between Jesus and his brothers (also mentioned in John 7.5)—a tension, however, that was evidently resolved after Jesus' resurrection (see 1 Cor. 15.7, Gal. 1.19; probably also Acts 12.17, 15.3).

[31] This statement in particular is implicit in Mark's comment, "And they were offended at him (καὶ ἐσκανδαλίζοντο ἐν αὐτῷ)" (6.3). The Greek text literally translated says that Jesus had become for them a "stumbling block"—on the implications of which see, e.g. 1 Peter 2.8.

## Act I – The Ministry of Jesus: in and around Galilee)

|  |  |
|---|---|
|  | And he called the twelve together and began to send them out two by two. |
| **Jesus:** | I give you authority over the unclean spirits. Take nothing for your journey except a staff. No bread, no bag, no money in your belts. You may wear sandals, but not two tunics. Where you enter a house, stay there until you leave the district. If any refuse to receive you or hear you, as you leave, shake the dust off your feet, as a witness against them. |
| **Evangelist 2:** | And they went out and made their proclamation. |
| **Disciples:** | *(different voices)* Turn back to God! |
|  | Turn back to God! |
| **Evangelist 2:** | They cast out many demons and anointed with oil many that were sick and healed them. |
|  | *Drumbeat* |
| **Evangelist 1:** | King Herod heard of it. For Jesus' name had become known. People were talking! |
| **Courtiers:** | *(several voices)* John the Baptizer has been raised from the dead! |
|  | That is why these powers are at work in him! |
|  | Elijah has returned! |
|  | It's a prophet, like one of the prophets of old. |
| **Evangelist 1:** | But then Herod heard about it. |
| **Herod Antipas:** | *(some anxiety, since he was responsible for John the Baptist's death)* It's John, whom I beheaded. He's been raised from the dead! |

| | |
|---|---|
| **Evangelist 1:** | For Herod had sent and arrested John and thrown him in gaol. He'd done this because of Herodias, his brother Philip's wife, whom he'd married. For John had said to Herod, "It's not lawful for you to have your brother's wife." So Herodias had a grudge against him and wanted to kill him. But she couldn't, because Herod was in awe of John, knowing he was a righteous and holy man. So he protected him. When he listened to him, he found him very troubling. And yet he liked listening to him. |
| **Evangelist 2:** | But finally Herodias got her chance! It was Herod's birthday. He gave a banquet for his top-ranking officials, military officers, and the leading men of Galilee. Then Herodias' daughter came in and danced. And Herod and his guests were delighted! |
| **Herod Antipas:** | Ask me whatever you wish, and I will grant it. *(With the emphasis of the somewhat inebriated)* I will grant it you, even to half of my kingdom! |
| **Evangelist 1:** | She went out to her mother. |
| **Salome:** | Mother, what should I ask for? |
| **Mother:** | The head of John the Baptizer! |
| **Evangelist 1:** | So she rushed straight back to the king. |
| **Salome:** | I want you to give me John the Baptist's head – on a platter! Now! |
| **Evangelist 1:** | The king was greatly upset. But because of his vows and his guests he couldn't bring himself to refuse her. So he sent a soldier with orders to bring John's head. The |

## Act I – The Ministry of Jesus: in and around Galilee

|  |  |
|---|---|
|  | soldier went and beheaded him in the prison, brought his head on a platter, and gave it to the girl. And the girl gave it to her mother. When John's disciples heard of it, they came and took his body and laid it in a tomb. |
|  | *Rattle* |
| **Evangelist 2:** | The apostles returned to Jesus and told him all that they had done and taught. |
| **Jesus:** | Come away by yourselves to somewhere peaceful. Let's get some rest. |
| **Evangelist 2:** | For many were coming and going, and they had no leisure even to eat. So, by themselves, they went away in the boat to a remote place. |
| **Evangelist 1:** | But lots of people had seen them setting out and recognized them. They rushed round on foot from all the towns and got there ahead of them. So when Jesus went ashore he was faced with a great crowd. |
| **Evangelist 2:** | And he pitied them. |
| **Jesus:** | They are like sheep without a shepherd. |
| **Evangelist 2:** | And he began to teach them. |
| **Evangelist 1:** | When it grew late, his disciples came to him. |
| **Disciples** | *(several voices):* Teacher, this is a lonely place. |
|  | And it's getting very late. |
|  | Send them away, so they can go into the country and local villages and buy themselves something to eat! |
| **Jesus:** | You give them something to eat. |

| | |
|---|---|
| **Disciples** | *(two voices)* Oh, yes! Right! We'll just go and buy a year's wages worth of bread, shall we? |
| | And give them that to eat? |
| **Jesus:** | How many loaves have you? Go and see. |
| **Evangelist 1:** | They went and found out. |
| **Disciples** | *(two voices)*: Five! |
| | And two fish! |
| **Jesus:** | All of you! Sit down in your groups on the grass. |
| **Evangelist 2:** | So they sat down in groups, by hundreds and by fifties. And taking the five loaves and the two fish he looked up to heaven, and blessed, and broke the loaves, and gave them to the disciples to set before the people. And he divided the two fish among them. And they all ate and were satisfied. And they filled twelve baskets with what was left of the bread and the fish. |
| **Evangelist 1:** | And those loaves fed about five thousand people. |
| | *(pause)* |
| | Immediately afterwards he made his disciples get into the boat and go before him to the other side, to Bethsaida, while he dismissed the crowd. And after he had taken leave of them, he went up into the mountains to pray. |
| | *Chime* |
| **Evangelist 2:** | When evening came, the boat was out on the sea, and he was alone on the land. He saw they were making |

## Act I – The Ministry of Jesus: in and around Galilee

|               | headway painfully, for the wind was against them. And about the fourth watch of the night he came to them, walking on the sea. |
|---|---|
| **Evangelist 1:** | Jesus meant to pass by them, but when they saw him walking on the sea, they thought it was a ghost and cried out. For they all saw him and were terrified. But then immediately he spoke to them. |
| **Jesus:** | Take heart! It is I! Don't be afraid. |
| **Evangelist 2:** | He got into the boat with them. And the wind ceased. And they were utterly astounded. For they did not understand about the loaves, but their heart was hardened. |

*Drumbeat*

**Evangelist 1:**  When they had crossed over they came to land at Gennesaret and there they made fast. When they came ashore, immediately people recognized him. They began bringing the sick on their pallets to any place where they heard he was. And wherever he came–in the villages or cities or farms–they would lay the sick in the market places and beg him that they might touch just the fringe of his garment. And as many as touched it were made well.

*Chime*

**Evangelist 1:**  A group of Pharisees and some scribes from Jerusalem met with him. They noticed that some of his disciples were eating with hands ritually unclean–that is, without washing them.

**Evangelist 2:** For the Pharisees [32] don't eat unless they wash their hands in the way prescribed for the ritual washing, [33] observing the tradition of the elders. And when they come from the market place, they don't eat unless they purify themselves. And there are many other traditions they observe, such as ritual washing of cups and pots and vessels of bronze.

**Evangelist 2:** So the Pharisees and scribes put a question to him.

**Pharisees:** Why do your disciples not walk[34] in the tradition of the elders? But eat with hands ritually unclean?

**Jesus:** How well Isaiah prophesied of you hypocrites!—as it is written, "This people honour me with their lips, but their heart is far from me! They worship me in vain, teaching human precepts as doctrines!" You give up on God's commandment and hold fast to human tradition! And how good at it you are! For Moses said, "Honour your father and your mother," and "He who speaks evil of his father or mother must die." But *you* say, "If a man tells his father or his mother, 'What you would have gained from me is *given to God*'" -- then you no longer permit him to do anything for his father or mother! So you make null and void the word of God! - through your tradition which you hand on. And you do many such things.

---

[32] Mark adds, "and all the Jews", which is certainly what some who advocated these practices claimed for them (e.g. *Letter of Aristeas* 305-307). They, however, and the evangelist, were factually incorrect, since the practices were not universal. Neither the common people nor the Sadducees will have observed them. So I have omitted the phrase: but it may, of course, be restored if the director wishes here to follow Mark exactly.

[33] By "in the way prescribed for the ritual washing" I paraphrase Mark's Greek, "πυγμῇ": literally "with the fist"—a technical expression which evidently did carry the force I have given it, but whose precise meaning is no longer clear: see e.g. Boring, *Mark* 199.

[34] The choice of expression probably reflects the term Halakah, traditionally associated with Hebrew *halak*–"to walk".

## Act I – The Ministry of Jesus: in and around Galilee

|  |  |
|---|---|
|  | *(turning to the entire community present)* |
|  | Hear me, all of you, and understand! There is nothing outside of you which by going into you can defile you. But the things that come out of a you—they are what defile you! |
| **Evangelist 1:** | When he had entered the house and left the people, his disciples asked him. |
| **Disciples:** | Teacher, tell us about the parable. What do you mean? |
| **Jesus:** | So even you don't understand? Can't you see that whatever goes into a man from outside cannot defile him, since it doesn't enter his heart but his stomach, and so passes on? |
| **Evangelist 2:** | Thus he declared all foods clean. |
| **Jesus:** | It's what comes out of you that defiles you. For from within, out of your heart, come evil thoughts, fornication, theft, murder, adultery, coveting, wickedness, deceit, licentiousness, envy, slander, pride, foolishness. All these evil things come from within, and they are what defile you! |
|  | *Drumbeat* |
| **Evangelist 2:** | From there he arose and went away to the region of Tyre. He was staying at a house and didn't want anyone to know it. But he couldn't escape notice. In no time a woman whose daughter was possessed by an unclean spirit heard about him. She came and fell at his feet. The woman was a Greek, a Syrophoenician by race. |
| **Syrophoenician Woman:** | Teacher, I beg you, cast the demon out of my daughter. |

| | |
|---|---|
| **Jesus:** | Let the children be fed first. It isn't right to take the children's food and give it to the dogs. |
| **Syrophoenician Woman:** | True, Lord. Yet even now, the dogs under the table do get to eat the children's crumbs. |
| | *(pause)* |
| **Jesus:** | For that Word, go your way. The demon has left your daughter.[35] |
| **Evangelist 1:** | She went home and found the child lying in bed, and the demon gone. |
| | *Chime.* |
| **Evangelist 2:** | Then he returned from the region of Tyre, and went through Sidon to the Sea of Galilee, through the region of the Decapolis. |
| | *Crowd noise in background:* |
| **Bystanders** | *(various voices):* Teacher, here's a man who's deaf. |
| | And he can't talk properly. |
| | Teacher, if you could just lay your hands on him– |
| **Jesus:** | I will. Let's bring him aside, away from this crowd. Along here! |
| | *Crowd noise dies way.* |

---

[35] Jesus did not begin life knowing everything, any more than he began life six feet tall. He had to learn (cf. Luke 2:52)–and this narrative, I believe, records such a learning moment (see further my *Mary of Nazareth*, 8, 162 n.3). I used, when I was teaching, to refer to this narrative as the one time in the gospel tradition where Jesus loses an argument–noting, incidentally, that it was to a woman and a foreigner. Despite some commentators, I do not believe that I was wrong. That Jesus could lose an argument was one sign of his true humanity. That he appeared to have not the slightest trouble admitting it was a sign that his humanity was perfect. .

## Act I – The Ministry of Jesus: in and around Galilee

**Evangelist 2:** Jesus put his fingers into the man's ears, and touched his tongue with spittle. Then he looked up to heaven, sighed, and spoke.

**Jesus:** *Ephphatha:* be opened!

**Evangelist 2:** And at once the man's ears were opened! His tongue was released! And he could speak clearly. Jesus charged them.

**Jesus:** Tell no one.

**Evangelist 2:** But the more he charged them, the more eagerly they proclaimed it, for they were utterly astounded–

**Other Bystanders:** *(various voices)*

He has done everything well.

He even makes the deaf hear!

And the mute speak!

*Chime*

**Evangelist 1:** Again, there was another time when a big crowd had gathered, and as they had nothing to eat, he called his disciples.

**Jesus:** I have compassion on the crowd. They've been with me now three days and have nothing to eat. If I send them home hungry, they'll faint on the way. And some of them have come a long way.

**Disciples** *(two voices)*: But how can we feed them here?

In the desert?

**Jesus:** How many loaves have you?

**Disciple:** Seven.

| | |
|---|---|
| **Jesus:** | Very well. *(calling out, as to the crowd)* All of you! My friends! Be seated! |
| **Evangelist 1:** | And he took the seven loaves. And having given thanks he broke them and gave them to his disciples to set before them, and they set them before the crowd. And they had a few small fish. And having blessed them, he commanded that these also should be set before them. And they ate and were satisfied. And they took up the broken pieces left over, seven baskets full. And there were about four thousand people. |
| **Jesus:** | And now, friends, go home! |
| | *Chime* |
| **Evangelist 2:** | And immediately he got into the boat with his disciples and went to the district of Dalmanutha. Pharisees came and began to argue with him, testing him. |
| **Pharisee:** | If the Kingdom is at hand, as you say, and you're a true prophet, then show us! Give us a sign from heaven! |
| **Jesus:** | *(sighs deeply)* Why does this generation seek a sign? Truly, I tell you, no sign at all will be given to this generation. |
| **Evangelist 2:** | And he left them, got back into the boat and departed to the other side of the lake. Now they'd forgotten to bring bread and—except for one loaf—had none with them in the boat. Jesus was teaching them: |
| **Jesus:** | Stay alert! Watch out for the leaven of the Pharisees and the leaven of Herod. |
| **Disciples** | *(different voices)*: What's he mean? |
| | Is this because we haven't any bread? |

Act I – The Ministry of Jesus: in and around Galilee

**Jesus:** *(wearily)* Why are you talking about not having bread? Do you still not understand? Are your hearts hardened? Having eyes do you not see, and having ears do you not hear? And don't you remember? When I broke the five loaves for the five thousand, how many baskets of broken pieces did you take up?

**Disciple:** Twelve.

**Jesus:** And the seven for the four thousand, how many baskets full of broken pieces did you take up?

**Disciple:** Seven.

**Jesus:** Do you still not understand?

*Drumbeat.*

# Act II

The Road to Jerusalem:
giving sight to the blind

(Mark 8.22-10.52)

| | |
|---|---|
| **Evangelist 1:** | Jesus and his disciples came to Bethsaida. And people brought to him a blind man and begged him to touch him. And he took the blind man by the hand and led him out of the village; and when he had spit on his eyes and laid his hands upon him, he asked him, |
| **Jesus:** | Do you see anything? |
| **Man:** | I see men; but they look like trees, walking. |
| **Evangelist 1:** | Then again he laid his hands upon his eyes; and he looked intently and was restored and saw everything clearly. |
| **Jesus:** | Go straight to your home. Don't even go into the village. |
| | *Drumbeat* |
| **Evangelist 1:** | And Jesus went on with his disciples to the villages of Caesarea Philippi. And on the way he questioned his disciples. |
| **Jesus:** | Who do people say that I am? |
| **Disciples** | *(several voices)* John the Baptist! |
| | Others say, Elijah! |
| | And others one of the prophets. |
| **Jesus:** | But you—who do you say that I am?" |
| **Evangelist 1:** | It was Peter who answered. |
| **Peter:** | You are the Messiah, God's anointed One. |
| **Jesus:** | Tell no one about me. |
| | *Drumbeat* |

## Act II – The Road to Jerusalem: giving sight to the blind

|  | The Son of man must suffer many things and be rejected by the elders and the chief priests and the scribes and be killed, and after three days rise again. |
|---|---|
| **Evangelist 1:** | And he was saying this quite frankly. But Peter took hold of him! |
| **Peter:** | God forbid, teacher! This shall never happen to you![36] |
| **Evangelist 1:** | Jesus turned and saw his disciples were watching. He said to Peter, |
| **Jesus:** | Get out of my way, Satan! You're not on God's side, but man's. |

*(to the audience)*

Listen, all of you. If any among you would be my followers, let them deny themselves and take up their cross and follow me. Those who want to save their life will lose it, and those who lose their life for my sake, and for the sake of the gospel, will save it. What will it profit them to gain the whole world and lose their life? Indeed, what can they give in exchange for their life? Those who are ashamed of me and my words in this adulterous and sinful generation, of them the Son of Man will be ashamed when he comes in the glory of his Father with the holy angels.

*Chime*

---

[36] Matthew 16.22! In following my usual practise of turning Mark's implied speech into direct speech where I can, it seemed foolish not to follow Mark's fellow evangelist where he has already done the job for me—save that I have changed Matthew's "Lord" to "teacher," since Peter never calls Jesus "Lord" in Mark's account, but he does call him "teacher" or "Rabbi" (e.g. 9.5).

|  |  |
|---|---|
| | Truly, I tell you, there are some standing here who will not taste death before they see the kingdom of God— come with power! |
| **Evangelist 1:** | Six days later Jesus took with him Peter and James and John, and led them up a high mountain, apart, by themselves. |
| **Peter:** | Look! Up ahead! What's happening to the teacher? |
| **James:** | His clothes, they're all white! |
| **John:** | He's... he's *shining*. He's *transfigured!* |
| **Peter:** | There's not a launderer on earth could get them like that. |
| **James:** | Who's he with? There's two of them. |
| **John:** | It's Elijah and Moses. They're talking with him. |
| **Peter:** | *(calls out, babbling)* Rabbi, it's good we're here! Let's make three booths! One for you! One for Moses! And one for Elijah! *(then conspiratorially, to James and John)* I don't know what to say. This is terrifying. |
| **Evangelist 1:** | A cloud overshadowed them: and out of the cloud, a voice: |
| **God:** | This is my Son, my beloved. Listen to him.[37] |
| **Evangelist 2:** | And suddenly, looking round, they saw there was no-one with them, only Jesus. |
| | *Chime* |

---

[37] These words (Mark 9.8) declare Jesus alone to be the one in whom Moses' propehecy at Deut. 18.15 is fulfilled.

Act II – The Road to Jerusalem: giving sight to the blind)

**Evangelist 1:** As they were coming back, down the mountain, Jesus gave them an order.

**Jesus:** Tell no one what you've seen, not until the Son of man has risen from the dead.

**James:** We'll keep it to ourselves, teacher.

**Peter:** But – what do you mean, about the Son of Man rising from the dead?

**John:** Don't the scribes say Elijah must come first?

**Jesus:** Does Elijah come first to restore all things? Then how is it written of the Son of Man that he should suffer much and be treated with contempt? I tell you, Elijah has indeed come, and they've done to him whatever they pleased, just as it is written of him.

*Drumbeat*

**Evangelist 1:** When they came to the disciples, they saw a great crowd round them, and scribes arguing with them. And immediately all the crowd, when they saw him, were astonished, and ran up and greeted him.

**Jesus:** What were you arguing about?

**Man from the crowd:** Teacher, I brought my son to you, for he has a dumb spirit. And wherever it seizes him, it dashes him down; and he foams and grinds his teeth and becomes rigid. And I asked your disciples to cast it out, and they couldn't.

**Jesus:** O faithless generation, how long am I to be with you? How long am I to bear with you? Bring him to me.

| | |
|---|---|
| **Evangelist 1:** | And they brought the boy to him; and when the spirit saw him, immediately it convulsed the boy, and he fell on the ground and rolled about, foaming at the mouth. |
| **Jesus:** | How long has he had this? |
| **Boy's father:** | From childhood. And it has often cast him into the fire and into the water, to destroy him; but if you can do anything, have pity on us and help us. |
| **Jesus:** | If you can! All things are possible to him who believes. |
| **Boy's Father** | *(crying out):* I do believe. Help my unbelief! |
| **Evangelist 1:** | When Jesus saw the crowd was closing in on them, he rebuked the unclean spirit. |
| **Jesus:** | You, dumb and deaf spirit, I command you, come out of him! And never enter him again! |
| **Evangelist 2:** | And after crying out and convulsing him terribly, it came out, and the boy was like a corpse. |
| **Bystanders** | *(various voices):* He's not moving. |
| | He's dead. |
| | Yeah, he's a goner all right. |
| **Evangelist 2:** | But Jesus took him by the hand. |
| **Jesus:** | *(gently)* Up you get, lad! That's it. |
| **Evangelist 2:** | And the boy got up! |
| | *Drumbeat* |
| | When Jesus went indoors, his disciples asked him. |
| **Disciple:** | Why couldn't we cast it out? |

Act II – The Road to Jerusalem: giving sight to the blind)

**Jesus:** This kind cannot be driven out by anything but prayer.

*Drumbeat.*

**Evangelist 2:** They went on from there and passed through Galilee. And he didn't want it known, for he was teaching his disciples.

**Jesus:** The Son of man will be delivered into the hands of men, and they will kill him; and when he is killed, after three days he will rise.

**Evangelist 2:** But they didn't understand what he was saying and were afraid to ask him.

*Drumbeat*

**Evangelist 1:** And they came to Capernaum. When he was indoors he put a question to them.

**Jesus:** What were you discussing on the road?

**Evangelist 1:** And they were silent. For on the road they'd been arguing with each other about who was the greatest. And he sat down and called the twelve. And he said to them:

**Jesus:** If any of you would be first, you must be last of all and servant of all.

**Evangelist 2:** He took a child, set him in the midst of them, and put his arm round him.

**Jesus:** Whoever receives one child such as this in my name receives me; and whoever receives me does not receive me but the one who sent me.

*Drumbeat*

**John:** Teacher, we saw a man casting out demons in your name, and we forbade him, because he wasn't with us.

| | |
|---|---|
| **Jesus:** | Don't forbid him. Whoever is not against us is for us. Whoever gives you a cup of water to drink because you belong to Christ, truly I tell you, they will not lose their reward. But whoever upsets the faith of one of these little ones who believe in me, it would have been better for them if a millstone had been hung round their neck and they they'd been flung into the sea. Salt is good; but if salt has lost its saltness, how will you season it? Have salt among yourselves and be at peace with one another. |
| | *Drumbeat* |
| **Evangelist 2:** | And he left there and went to the region of Judea and beyond the Jordan, and crowds gathered to him again; and again, as his custom was, he taught them. And Pharisees came to test him. |
| **Pharisee:** | Tell us, teacher, is it lawful for a man to put away his wife? |
| **Jesus:** | *(wearily?)* What did Moses command you? |
| **Pharisee:** | Moses allowed a man to write a certificate of divorce, and to put her away. |
| **Jesus:** | He wrote this commandment for you because of your hardness of heart. But from the beginning of creation, "God made them male and female... For this reason a man shall leave his father and mother and be joined to his wife, and the two shall become one flesh." So they're no longer two but one flesh. What God has joined together, a mere human being ought not to put asunder. |
| | *Drumbeat* |

## Act II – The Road to Jerusalem: giving sight to the blind

**Evangelist 1:** And they were bringing children to him, that he might touch them; and the disciples rebuked them. But when Jesus saw it he was indignant.

**Jesus:** Let the children come to me! Do not stop them! God's kingdom belongs to such as these. Truly, I tell you, whoever doesn't receive the kingdom of God like a child shall never enter it.

**Evangelist 1:** And he took the children in his arms and blessed them and laid his hands on them.

*Drumbeat*

**Evangelist 2:** As he was setting out, a man ran up and knelt before him.

**Man:** Good Teacher, what must I do to inherit eternal life?

**Jesus:** Why do you call me good? No one is good but God alone. You know the commandments: "Do not kill, Do not commit adultery, Do not steal, Do not bear false witness, Do not defraud, Honor your father and mother."

**Man:** Teacher, all these I have observed from my youth.

**Jesus:** *(warmly, gently)* You lack one thing. Go, sell what you have, and give to the poor, and you will have treasure in heaven. And come, follow me.

**Evangelist 2:** At that saying his countenance fell, and he went away sorrowful; for he had great possessions. Jesus looked at his disciples.

**Jesus:** How hard it will be for people with riches to enter the kingdom of God!

Dramatic Mark: The Gospel according to St Mark

**Evangelist 2:** His disciples were amazed at this.

**Jesus:** Children, how hard it is to enter the kingdom of God! It is easier for a camel to go through the eye of a needle than for the rich to enter the kingdom of God.

**Disciple:** Then who can be saved?[38]

**Jesus:** For mere mortals it's impossible, but not for God! All things are possible with God.

**Peter:** What about us? We've left everything to follow you—

**Jesus:** Truly I tell you, there's no one who has left house or brothers or sisters or mother or father or children or lands, for my sake and for the gospel, who will not, even in this age, receive a hundred times as much—houses and brothers and sisters and mothers and children and lands—with persecutions! And in the age to come, eternal life! But many so called "first" will be last, and the last first.

*Chime*

**Evangelist 1:** They were on the road, going up to Jerusalem. And Jesus was striding ahead of them.

**Disciples:** *(various male voices):* I don't understand.

What's got into him?

I don't know.

**Other followers of Jesus:** *(various voices, female or male):* He's scaring me.[39]

Me too.

---

[38] For once the disciples understand! There are many kinds of "riches" besides material wealth. But none of these, in themselves, will save us. In what follows Jesus indicates that to follow him is, even in the present life, to become part of something bigger and richer than any human wealth or family, although it is also to face persecution.

## Act II – The Road to Jerusalem: giving sight to the blind

**Evangelist 2:** Again Jesus took the twelve aside.

**Jesus:** Listen. We are going up to Jerusalem. And the Son of man will be handed over to the chief priests and the scribes, and they will condemn him to death, and hand him over to the Gentiles. And they will mock him and spit on him and beat him and scourge him and kill him. And after three days he will rise again.

*Drumbeat*

**Evangelist 1:** James and John, Zebedee's sons, come up to him.

**James:** Teacher!

**John:** Teacher, we want you to do for us whatever we ask!

**Jesus:** What do you want me to do for you?

**James:** Grant us to sit, one at your right hand . . . .

**John:** . . . and one at your left, in your glory.

**Jesus:** You don't know what you are asking. Are you able to drink the cup that I drink, or to be baptized with the baptism with which I am baptized?

**James:** We are.

---

[39] Following the statement that Jesus was going ahead of them, Mark says, "καὶ ἐθαμβοῦντο, οἱ δὲ ἀκολουθοῦντες ἐφοβοῦντο"– which might be literally translated: "and they were amazed, but those following were afraid"–possibly implying a distinction between two groups? Perhaps the women who followed Jesus (to whom Mark will refer directly at 15.41) were among the group that were quicker than the twelve (male) disciples to perceive the danger ahead? Such a distinction between the Twelve and other followers of Jesus may be implicit in Mark's Greek and intended by him (cf. Cranfield, *Mark* 335), and in rendering the passage into direct discourse, by atttributing the latter remarks to "Other followers", I allow for that distinction. The director could cast these with women's voices. There is, of course, nothing strange in this mixture of wonder and fear among Jesus' followers, as he proceeds into what is evidently a dangerous situation.

**John:** We can do it.

**Jesus:** The cup that I drink you will drink. And you will be baptized with the baptism with which I am baptized. But to sit at my right hand or my left—that's not mine to give. It's for those for whom it's been prepared.

**Evangelist 1:** When the ten heard about all this, they started getting angry with James and John. Jesus calls the group to him.

**Jesus:** You know those reckoned to be "rulers" among the Gentiles lord it over them, and their great ones enforce their authority. It is not to be like that among you. But whoever wants to be great among you will be your servant, and whoever wants to be first among you will be everyone's slave. For the Son of man also came not to be served but to serve, and to give his life as a ransom for many.

*Chime.*

**Evangelist 2:** They come to Jericho. And as he was leaving the town with his disciples and a great crowd, Bartimaeus, a blind beggar, son of Timaeus,[40] was sitting by the roadside.

**Bartimaeus:** What's all the fuss about? What's going on?

**Crowd** *(various voices):* It's him, Bartimaeus! Jesus of Nazareth!

He's going by now!

---

[40] Is Mark again speaking of a known eyewitness (so Cranfield, *Mark* 344)? The oddity in Bartimaeus' expression – that he calls Jesus "Son of David" rather than "teacher" as is more usual in Mark's narrative – in my view tells for rather than against this possibility (against Bultmann, *Synoptic Tradition* 213).

Act II – The Road to Jerusalem: giving sight to the blind)

**Bartimaeus:** *(muttering to himself)* Jesus of Nazareth! He could heal me. *(out loud, shouting)* Jesus, Son of David, have mercy on me! Have mercy on me!

**Crowd** *(various voices):* For God's sake man, shut up!

He's got more important things to worry about than you!

**Bartimaeus:** Son of David, have mercy on me!

**Crowd** *(various voices):* Wait a minute though—he's stopping!

He's looking round!

**Jesus:** Call him.

**Crowd** *(various voices):* Go for it, man!

Get up!

He's calling you!

**Evangelist 1:** So Bartimaeus threw off his cloak, got up and came to Jesus.

**Jesus:** What do you want me to do for you?

**Bartimaeus:** Oh, teacher, I want to see!

**Jesus:** *(gently)* Then so be it! Your faith has healed you!

**Evangelist 1:** And at once he received his sight! And he followed him on the way.

*Drumbeat.*

# Act III

In and around Jerusalem

# Scene 1. Teaching (Mark 11.1–15.47)

**Evangelist 2:** As they are approaching Jerusalem, at Bethphagé[41] and Bethany, near the Mount of Olives, Jesus sends two of his disciples ahead.

**Jesus:** Go into the village opposite. As soon as you enter it you'll find a colt tied. He's never been ridden. Untie him and bring him to me. If someone says, "What are you doing?" just say, "The colt's Master needs him. And he'll send him back soon."

**Evangelist 2:** So they went away, and found a colt tethered by a doorway in the open street. And as they're untying it –

**People:** *(several voices)* What are you doing?

Why are you untying the colt?

**Disciples:** The colt's Master needs him. And he'll send him back soon.

**People:** *(several voices)* Oh, all right then.

Off you go, lads!

**Evangelist 2:** They bring the colt to Jesus, and throw their cloaks on it, and he sat on it. And many were spreading their cloaks on the road, and others were scattering palm branches cut from the fields. And those going ahead and those following were shouting!

**People** *(several voices): (general cheers and applause)*
Hosanna!

Blessed who comes in the name of the Lord!

Hosanna! Hosanna!

---

[41] "Bethfagé" has three syllables, is accented on the first syllable, and the "g" is hard.

## Act III – In and around Jerusalem

|  | Blessed the coming kingdom of our father David! Hosanna in the highest! Hosanna! |
|---|---|
| **Evangelist 2:** | And he entered Jerusalem and went into the temple. And when he'd looked round at everything, since it was already late, he went out to Bethany with the twelve. |
|  | *Drumbeat* |
| **Evangelist 1:** | Next day, after they'd left Bethany, he was hungry. And seeing some way off a fig tree in leaf, he went to see if he could find anything on it. When he came to it, he found nothing but leaves, for it wasn't the season for figs. |
| **Jesus:** | May no one ever eat fruit from you again. |
| **Evangelist 1:** | And his disciples heard it. |
|  | *Drumbeat* |
| **Evangelist 2:** | And they come to Jerusalem. And he entered the temple and began to drive out those who sold and those who bought in the temple, and he overturned the tables of the money-changers and the seats of those who sold pigeons; and he would allow no one to carry anything through the temple. |
| **Jesus:** | Is it not written, "My house shall be called a house of prayer for all the nations"? But you have made it a den of thieves! |
| **Evangelist 2:** | And the chief priests and the scribes heard it and they were looking for a way to make an end of him. They regarded him as dangerous, for the crowds were spellbound by his teaching. |
|  | *(pause)* |
|  | And when it was evening, Jesus and those who were following him left the city. |
|  | *Drumbeat* |

| | |
|---|---|
| **Evangelist 1:** | In the morning, as they were passing by, they saw the fig tree withered to its roots. And Peter remembered. |
| **Peter:** | Rabbi, look! The fig tree you cursed has withered. |
| **Jesus:** | Have faith in God. Truly I tell you, whoever says to this mountain, "Be taken up and cast into the sea," and does not doubt in their heart but believes that what they are saying will happen, it will be done for them. So I say to you, whatever you ask in prayer, believe that you have received it, and it will happen for you. And whenever you stand praying, if you have anything against any one, forgive them, so that your Father in heaven may forgive your trespasses, too. |
| | *Drumbeat* |
| **Evangelist 2:** | And they came again to Jerusalem. As he was walking in the temple, the chief priests and the scribes and the elders came to him. |
| **Scribes** | *(two voices)*: So—by what authority are you acting in this way? |
| | Who gave you this authority? |
| **Jesus:** | I will ask you a question. Answer me, and I will tell you by what authority I act. The baptism of John! – was it from heaven? or merely human?[42] Answer me. |
| | *(silence – then)* |
| **Priests, scribes and elders:** | *(talking among themselves: several voices):* If we say, "From heaven," he'll say, "Then why didn't you believe him? |

---

[42] The question is more than a ploy: John's and Jesus' ministries were linked. If one was valid, so was the other.

## Act III – In and around Jerusalem

|  | But if we say, "Of human origin"? |
|---|---|
|  | There'll be trouble! |
|  | This mob thinks John was really a prophet! |
|  | *(finally, one of them, to Jesus)* We don't know. |
| **Jesus:** | Then neither am I telling you by what authority I do these things. |
|  | *Drumbeat* |
| **Listen!** | Listen! man planted a vineyard, and set a hedge round it, and dug a pit for the wine press, and built a tower, and let it out to tenants, and went into another country. When the time came, he sent a servant to the tenants, to get from them some of the fruit of the vineyard. And they took him and beat him and sent him away empty-handed. Again he sent to them another servant, and they wounded him in the head and treated him shamefully. And he sent another, and they killed him! And so with many others, some they beat and some they killed. He had still one other, a beloved son. Finally he sent him to them, saying, "They will respect my son." But those tenants said to one another, "This is the heir; come, let us kill him, and the inheritance will be ours." And they took him and killed him and cast him out of the vineyard. What will the owner of the vineyard do? |
| **Bystanders** | *(various voices):* He'll come and destroy the tenants. |
|  | He'll give the vineyard to some as deserve it! |
| **Jesus:** | Have you never read this scripture: "The very stone which the builders rejected has become the head of the corner. This was the Lord's doing, and it is marvellous in our eyes"? |

| | |
|---|---|
| **Evangelist 1:** | The priests wanted to arrest him, for they knew he'd told the parable against them. But they feared the crowd, so they left him and went away. |
| | *Drumbeat* |
| **Evangelist 2:** | Some Pharisees and Herodians were sent to entrap him with a question. |
| **Pharisees and Herodians** | *(various voices):* Teacher, we know that you are true. And you don't care what anyone thinks. |
| | For you don't take any notice of what people think, but truly teach God's ways. |
| | So—is it permitted to pay taxes to Caesar, or not? |
| | Should we pay, or no? |
| **Jesus:** | Why are you testing me? Bring me a denarius! Show it me! |
| | *(Pause). They show him the coin.* |
| **Jesus:** | Whose image and inscription is this? |
| **Pharisees and Herodians** | *(various voices):* Caesar's. |
| | Caesar's, of course. |
| **Jesus:** | Then pay to Caesar what belongs to Caesar—and to God what belongs to God. |
| **Evangelist 2:** | And they were stunned by his response. |
| | *Drumbeat* |
| **Evangelist 1:** | Sadducees came to him, who say that there is no resurrection. |
| **Sadducees** | *(several voices):* Teacher, Moses wrote for us that if a man's brother dies and leaves a wife, but leaves no child, |

## Act III – In and around Jerusalem

the man must take the wife and raise up children for his brother.

Well, there were seven brothers.

The first took a wife, and when he died he left no children.

And the second took her, and he died, and *he* left no children.

And the third–just the same!

And the seven–they *all* left no children!

Last of all the woman died.

Now, teacher, in the–er–*resurrection*, whose wife will she be? For the seven had her as wife!

**Jesus:** Is not this why you are wrong? Because you know neither the scriptures nor the power of God! When they rise from the dead, they neither marry nor are they given in marriage, but are like angels in heaven. As for the dead being raised, have you never read in the book of Moses, in the passage about the bush, how God said to Moses, "I am the God of Abraham, and the God of Isaac, and the God of Jacob"? He is not God of the dead, but of the living! You are utterly wrong.

*Drumbeat*

**Evangelist 1:** One of the scribes came up and heard them disputing with one another, and seeing that he answered them well, asked him a question.

**Scribe:** Teacher, which commandment is the first of all?

**Jesus:** The first is, "Hear, O Israel: The Lord our God, the Lord is one; and you shall love the Lord your God with all your heart, and with all your soul, and with all your mind, and with all your strength." The second is this, "You shall love your neighbour as yourself." There is no other commandment greater than these."

**Scribe:** You are right, Teacher. You have truly said that he is one, and there is no other but he. And to love him with all the heart, and with all the understanding, and with all the strength, and to love one's neighbour as oneself, is much more than all whole burnt offerings and sacrifices.

**Jesus:** You have answered wisely. You are not far from the kingdom of God.

**Evangelist 1:** And after that no one dared ask him any question.

*Drumbeat*

**Evangelist 2:** Jesus continued teaching in the temple.

**Jesus:** How can the scribes say that the Messiah, God's anointed, is "son of David"? David himself, inspired by the Holy Spirit, said, "The Lord said to my Lord, Sit at my right hand, till I put thy enemies under thy feet." David himself calls him Lord. So how is he his son?

*Drumbeat*

Act III – In and around Jerusalem

## Scene II. Jesus' final public teaching and farewell.

**Evangelist 2:** Huge crowds were listening to Jesus eagerly! And as he taught them, he said:

**Jesus:** Beware of the scribes, who like to go about in long robes and have salutations in the market places and the best seats in the synagogues and the places of honour at feasts, who devour widows' houses and for a pretence make long prayers. They will receive the greater condemnation.

**Evangelist 1:** He sat down opposite the treasury and watched the crowds putting money in. Many rich people put in large sums. And a poor widow came and put in two copper coins. Jesus called his disciples.

**Jesus:** Truly I tell you, this poor widow has put in more than all of them. They all contributed out of their abundance. But she out of her poverty has put in everything she had, her whole living!

*Drumbeat*

**Evangelist 1:** As he came out of the temple, one of his disciples said to him,

**Disciple:** Look, Teacher, what wonderful stones and what wonderful buildings!

**Jesus:** You see these great buildings? There won't be one stone here left standing on another. They'll all be thrown down.

**Evangelist 1:** And as he sat on the Mount of Olives opposite the temple, Peter and James and John and Andrew asked him privately.

**Peter:** Tell us, when will this be?

**James:** What'll be the sign when all these things are going to happen?

**Jesus:** Be on your guard. Don't let anyone mislead you. Many will come, claiming to be sent by me, saying, "I'm the one!"—and many will be misled by them. And when you hear of wars and rumours of wars, don't be alarmed! This must take place, but the end isn't yet. For nation will rise against nation and kingdom against kingdom. There'll be earthquakes. There'll be famines. This is the beginning of birth-pangs.

Watch out for yourselves! They'll hand you over to councils. You'll be beaten in synagogues. And for my sake you will stand before governors and kings to bear witness. And the gospel must first be preached to all nations. When they bring you to trial, don't be anxious what you are to say. Say whatever's given you in that hour, for it isn't you speaking, it's the Holy Spirit.

Brother will hand over brother to death, and a father his child. Children will turn against their parents and have them put to death. Everyone will hate you because you follow me. But those who endure to the end will be saved.

When you see the "abomination of desolation"[43] usurping a place that doesn't belong to it, then those who are in Judea should flee to the mountains. Don't anyone on the roof go down into the house to get

---

[43] The expression comes from Daniel 12.11: but use of it here plainly indicates that its significance is not exhausted. The right-wing nationalism and xenophobia that will lead to the War of AD 66-70, which in its turn will lead to the destruction of the Temple in 70, will be manifestations of the very same spirit of profanation.

something! Don't anyone in the field go back to fetch a cloak! Alas for those with child or giving suck in those days! Pray it doesn't happen in winter.

And if any one says to you, "Look, here is the Messiah!" or "Look, there he is!" don't believe it. False messiahs and false prophets will appear and show signs and wonders to lead astray, if possible, even the elect. Be careful! I've told you everything before it happens.

In those days, after that tribulation, the sun will be darkened, and the moon will not give its light. The stars will be falling from heaven, and the powers in the heavens will be shaken. And then they will see the Son of Man coming in clouds with great power and glory. And he will send out the angels, and gather his elect from the four winds, from the ends of the earth to the ends of heaven.

From the fig tree learn its lesson: as soon as its branch becomes tender and puts forth its leaves, you know that summer is near. So also, when you see these things happening, you know that he is near, at the very gates.

Truly, I tell you, this generation will not pass away before these things happen.

Heaven and earth will pass away,[44] but my words will not pass away. But of that day or hour no one knows, not even the angels in heaven, nor the Son, but only the Father.

---

[44] Jesus has spoken of the coming siege and destruction of Jerusalem, and now moves on to speaking about God's final judgment of the world at the end of time: a "day" and "hour" as yet unknown to the angels and even to Jesus himself.

Be alert! Watch! For you do not know when the time will come. It's like a man going on a journey. He leaves home and puts his servants in charge, each with his own work, and orders the doorkeeper to be on the lookout. Watch therefore! – for you do not know when the master of the house will come: in the evening, or at midnight, or at cockcrow, or in the morning–lest he come suddenly and find you asleep!

And what I say to you disciples I say to all: Watch!

*Drumbeat*

**Evangelist 1:**[45] It was now two days before Passover, and the festival of Unleavened Bread. The chief priests and the scribes were looking for a way to arrest Jesus by stealth and kill him.

**High Priest:** But not during the festival!

**A Scribe:** There could be a riot!

*Rattle*

**Evangelist 2:** While Jesus was in Bethany at Simon the leper's house, while he was at the table, a woman came in with an alabaster jar of very expensive perfume, pure oil of nard. And she broke open the jar and poured the oil on his head.

**Evangelist 1:** But some there were offended!

**Bystanders** *(various voices):* Why was the oil wasted like this?

This oil could have been sold for more than three hundred denarii and the money given to the poor!

---

[45] In what follows, I am indebted to David Landon for permission to draw on the version of Mark 14.1-15.47 prepared by him for the University of the South Theatre Department's presentation of Mark's passion narrative in All Saints' Chapel, Sewanee, on the appropriate Palm Sundays during the early 2000s.

Act III – In and around Jerusalem

It's ridiculous waste!

Woman, you ought to be ashamed of yourself!

**Jesus** *(strong and firm, cutting across them):* Let her alone! Why are you harassing her? She has done me a great kindness. You always have the poor with you, and whenever you want you can do good for them. But you will not always have me. She has done what she could. She has anointed my body beforehand for burial. Truly I tell you, wherever the good news is proclaimed in the whole world, what she has done will be told in remembrance of her.

*Chime*

# Scene III    Jesus' passion, death, and burial

**Evangelist 1:**    Then Judas Iscariot, one of the twelve, went to the chief priests to betray him.

*Rattle*

**Evangelist 2:**    When they heard it, they were pleased and promised him money. So he began looking for an opportunity to betray him.

*Rattle*

**Evangelist 1:**    It was the first day of Unleavened Bread, when the Passover lamb is sacrificed. His disciples asked:

**Disciple:**    Where do you want us to go and prepare for you to eat Passover?

**Jesus:**    Go into the city, and a man carrying a water jar will meet you. Follow him! Wherever he enters, say to the owner, "The Teacher is asking, Where is my guest room, where I can eat Passover with my disciples?" He will show you a large room upstairs, furnished and ready. Prepare for us there.

**Evangelist 2:**    So the disciples set out and went to the city. They found everything as Jesus had told them and they prepared the Passover.

**Evangelist 1:**    When it was evening, he came with the twelve. When they had taken their places and were eating, Jesus spoke to them.

**Jesus:**    Truly I tell you, one of you will betray me. One who is eating with me!

## Act III – In and around Jerusalem

**Disciples:** *(various voices, very distressed):* God forbid!

It won't be me, teacher!

Nor me!

It surely won't be me!

**Jesus:** *(cutting quietly but firmly across them)* One of you twelve! One who is dipping bread into the bowl with me! The Son of Man goes as it is written of him, but woe to the one who betrays him! It would have been better for him if he had never been born.

*Drumbeat*

**Evangelist 1:** While they were eating, he took a loaf. After blessing it he broke it and gave it to them.

**Jesus:** Take it; this is my body.

**Evangelist 2:** Then he took a cup, and after giving thanks he gave it to them, and all of them drank from it.

**Jesus:** This is my blood of the covenant, which is poured out for many. Truly I tell you, I will never again drink of the fruit of the vine until that day when I drink it new in the kingdom of God.

*Chime*

**Evangelist 1:** When they had sung the hymn, they went out to the Mount of Olives.

**Jesus:** You will all abandon me; For it is written, "I will strike the shepherd, and the sheep will be scattered." *(pause: then very emphatically)* But after I am raised up, I will go before you to Galilee.

**Peter:** Even if they all abandon you, I won't.

| | |
|---|---|
| **Jesus:** | Oh Peter, truly I tell you, today, this very night, before the cock crows twice, you will deny me three times. |
| **Peter** | *(vehemently):* Even if I have to die with you, I will never deny you. |
| **Other disciples** | *(various voices):* None of us will! |
| | Never, teacher! |
| | Never! |
| | *Drumbeat* |
| **Evangelist 1:** | They went out to a place called Gethsemane. |
| **Jesus:** | Sit here while I pray. |
| **Evangelist 1:** | He took with him Simon Peter and James and John. |
| **Jesus:** | My heart is breaking. Simon, James, John—stay here. Stay awake. Watch. |
| | *Drumbeat* |
| **Evangelist 2:** | Going a little farther, he threw himself on the ground and prayed that if it were possible the hour might pass from him. |
| **Jesus:** | Abba, Father, for you all things are possible. Take this cup from me. Yet, not what I want, but what you want. |
| | *Chime* |
| **Evangelist 1:** | He came to the disciples and found them sleeping. |
| **Jesus:** | Simon, are you asleep? Couldn't you watch one hour? Keep awake and pray you don't come to the time of trial. The spirit indeed is willing, but the flesh is weak. |
| | *Chime* |

## Act III – In and around Jerusalem

**Evangelist 1:** And again he went away and prayed the same prayer. And once more he came and found them sleeping, for their eyes were very heavy. And they didn't know what to say to him.

**Evangelist 2:** He came a third time.

**Jesus:** Still sleeping? Still taking a rest? *(soft drumbeat and sound of men's voices approaching)* Enough! The hour has come. Look! The Son of Man is betrayed into the hands of sinners. Get up. Let's go. See, my betrayer is here!

*Drumbeat continues.*

**Evangelist 1:** Immediately, while he was still speaking, Judas, one of the twelve, arrived . . .

**Evangelist 2:** And with him a crowd with swords and clubs from the chief priests, the scribes, and the elders.

*Drumbeat stops!*

**Evangelist 1:** Now the traitor had given them a sign.

**Judas:** The man I kiss is the one you want. Arrest him and get him away safely.

*Rattle*

**Evangelist 1:** So when he came, he went up at once to Jesus—

**Judas:** Teacher!

**Evangelist 1:** —and kissed him. Then they laid hands on him and arrested him.

**Evangelist 2:** But one of those who was standing near drew his sword and struck the slave of the high priest, cutting off his ear.

| | |
|---|---|
| **Jesus:** | Have you come out with swords and clubs to arrest me as though I were a bandit? Day after day I was with you, teaching in the temple, and you did not arrest me. But let the scriptures be fulfilled. |
| **Evangelist 1 and 2 together:** | And abandoning him the disciples fled—all of them! |
| | *Drumbeat.* |
| | *The two evangelists look at each other for a moment, and then* **Evangelist 2 (Mark)** *continues:* |
| **Evangelist 2:** | There was a lad who'd followed Jesus and the rest of them from the house, wearing nothing but his loin cloth. They caught him!—but he gave them the slip, leaving the loin cloth behind, and ran off back home naked! |
| | *Drumbeat* |
| **Evangelist 1:** | They took Jesus to the high priest. And all the chief priests, the elders and the scribes were assembled. |
| **Evangelist 2:** | Peter followed him at a distance, right into the high priest's courtyard. And he was sitting with the guards, warming himself by the fire. |
| **Evangelist 1:** | Now the chief priests and the whole council were doing their best to find evidence against Jesus that would warrant a death sentence. But they found nothing. |
| **Evangelist 2:** | For many offered false testimony against him, but their statements didn't agree. |
| **Council member 1:** | We heard him say, "I'll destroy the Temple." |
| **Council Member 2:** | *(correcting previous speaker)* He said he'd destroy the Temple *made with hands.* |
| **Council Member 3:** | The point is, he claimed *he* was going to build *another* temple! |

Act III – In and around Jerusalem

**Council Member 4:** In three days!

**Council Member 2:** Yes, but he said he'd build that *without* hands.

**High Priest:** *(clearly exasperated)* So even on this point, your testimony isn't consistent!

**Evangelist 1:** Then the high priest stood up in the middle of them all.

**High Priest:** Jesus of Nazareth, have you nothing to say?

*Silence.*

**High Priest:** How do you answer these accusations?

*Silence*

**High Priest:** *(changing tactic)* Are you the Messiah, the Son of the Blessed?

**Jesus:** [46] I am. And you will see the Son of Man seated at the right hand of Power and coming with the clouds of heaven.

**Evangelist 2:** At which the high priest tore his robes!

**High Priest:** *(enraged)* Why do we still need witnesses? You have heard the blasphemy! What is your decision?

**Single Council member** *(quietly, matter-of-factly):* He should die.

**Another council member** *(slightly louder, more excited):* Death for his blasphemy!

**Third member:** Death!

**Two or three:** Death!

**Many male voices:** Death. Death. Death.

---

[46] It was not blasphemous to claim to be the Lord's anointed. It is Jesus' words which follow that are blasphemous—unless, of course, they make a claim that is true.

| | |
|---|---|
| **Evangelist 1:** | Some began to spit on him! |
| **Evangelist 2:** | To blindfold him! |
| **Evangelist 1:** | To strike him! |
| **Council Member:** | So prophesy, prophet! |
| **Second Council Member:** | Prophesy! |
| **Third Council Member:** | Prophesy! |
| **Evangelist 2:** | The guards also took him over and beat him. |
| | *Drumbeat. Silence.* |
| **Evangelist 1** | *(taking up the story):* Meanwhile, Peter was below in the courtyard. One of the high-priest's servant-girls came by. She saw Peter warming himself and stared at him. |
| **Servant-girl:** | You! You were with the Nazarene—with Jesus! |
| **Peter:** | *(mumbling)* What? Me? I–I don't know what you're talking about. |
| **Evangelist 1:** | And he went out into the forecourt. The servant-girl saw him there and started again. |
| **Servant-girl:** | He's one of them, you know! He's with the Nazarene! |
| **Peter:** | *(more loudly)* No. No! I'm most certainly not. |
| **Evangelist 1:** | But again, after a while, people who were standing around spoke up. |
| **Bystander:** | Of course you're one of them! |
| **Second Bystander:** | You're a Galilean! |
| **Peter:** | *(shouting)* Damn and blast you, man! I don't even know the fellow you're talking about. |

### Act III – In and around Jerusalem

*A cock crows.*

**Peter:** *(to himself, appalled)* Oh, dear God! He told me! Before the cock crows twice, you'll deny me three times. Oh, dear God, what have I done? *(weeps)*

*Drumbeat*

**Evangelist 2:** As soon as it was morning, the chief priests held a consultation with the elders and scribes and the whole council. They bound Jesus, led him away, and handed him over to Pilate for questioning.

**Pilate** *(very much the examining colonial magistrate of a great empire):* Are you then the "King of the Jews"?

**Jesus:** You are the one saying it.

**High Priest:** This fellow threatened to destroy the Temple.

**Other Priests** *(two voices):* He's deliberately provoking a breach of the peace.

A riot.

**Pilate:** Well, prisoner? You hear the accusations. What have you to say?

*Silence*

Nothing? No reply? You astonish me.

*Drumbeat*

**Evangelist 1:** Now it was Pilate's custom at the festival to release a prisoner for them, anyone they asked.

**Evangelist 2:** There was a man called Barabbas who was in prison with the rebels. They'd committed murder during the insurrection.

*Crowd noise begins and continues under what follows.*

| | |
|---|---|
| **Aide to Pilate:** | There's a crowd here, sir. They want to know if you're going to do the usual. |
| **Member of Crowd:** | *(shouting over the crowd)* What about it governor? It's festival time! |
| **Pilate:** | Do you want me to release the "King of the Jews" for you?' *(to his aide)* It's obvious the priests have only handed him over because they're jealous of him. |
| **Aide:** | I agree, sir. But I'm afraid they've stirred up the mob, too. |
| | *Crowd noise rises.* |
| **Man in Crowd:** | Free Barabbas! |
| **Others in Crowd** | *(various voices, male and female):* We want Barabbas! |
| | Barabbas! |
| | Barabbas! |
| | Good old Barabbas! |
| **Pilate:** | Then what do you want me to do with the man you call "King of the Jews?" |
| **Another Man in Crowd:** | Crucify him, governor! *(laughter)* |
| **Pilate:** | Why do that? |
| **A couple of voices from Crowd:** | *(louder and now more hostile)* Crucify him! |
| | Crucify him! |
| **Pilate:** | What crime has he committed? |
| **More voices from the Crowd** | *(as other members of the mob catch on—or think they do—and join in, quickly developing into a chant):* |
| | Crucify him! |

## Act III – In and around Jerusalem

|  |  |
|---|---|
|  | Crucify him! |
| **Aide** | *(the crowd is still chanting):* Sir, if you don't do something there's going to be a riot. |
| **Pilate:** | You're right. *(to the crowd, loudly)* Enough! *(sudden silence: after all, he does represent the Roman power)* Barabbas is released. |
| **Crowd:** | *(Cheers and shouts of approval.)* "Good old Barabbas!" |
|  | He's our man! |
| **Pilate:** | *(aside to his Aide)* As for Jesus of Nazareth, I'm not risking a riot.[47] Flogging and crucifixion. See to it. |
| **Aide:** | Yes sir. |
| **Evangelist 2:** | Then the soldiers led Jesus into the courtyard of the Praetorium–the Governor's residence—and they call together the whole cohort. |
| **Evangelist 1:** | They dressed him in a purple cloak; and twisting some thorns into a crown, they put it on him. |
| **One of the Soldiers:** | Now this here's a king! Show some respect, lads! |
| **Optio** | *(2nd in command after the centurion: loud, strong and brutal)* That's right! Bit of respect! Hail, King of the Jews! |

---

[47] In fairness to Pilate, it should be remembered that while one part of his job was to uphold Roman law (which he here failed to do) the other part (and some might have argued, the most important part) was to maintain the peace, and his resources for doing that were extremely limited. The only troops under his direct command were auxiliaries. The nearest regular frontline troops—legionaries—were in Syria, several hundred kilometres away. I have written further elswhere on the situation facing Pilate (and, indeed, the Sanhedrin) at this point: see my *Render to Caesar*, 55-64, 68-75.

| | |
|---|---|
| **Soldiers:** | (*male voices gradually joining in and becoming rhythmic: they are deliberately parodying the "Hail Caesar" salute with which they would acknowledge the Emperor*): Hail, King! Hail, King! Hail, King! Hail, King! (*dissolving into raucous laughter: over which the evangelist speaks*) |
| **Evangelist 2:** | They beat his head with a stick and spat at him and knelt down in homage. |
| **Soldiers** | (*various male voices, tumbling over each other*): Oh, great king! |
| | Noble king! |
| | Hear us, oh king! |
| **Evangelist 1:** | After mocking him, they stripped him of the cloak and put his own clothes on him– |
| **Evangelist 2:** | – and led him out to crucify him. |
| | *Rattle* |
| **Evangelist 1:** | Now there was a passerby coming in from outside the city. |
| **Centurion:** | Hey you! You're a big strong lad. I've got a job for you.[48] |
| **Evangelist 2:** | It was Simon of Cyrene (*Mark points to Alexander and Rufus, who are among the readers*) Alexander's and Rufus's dad.[49] (*They nod in acknowledgment*) And they make him carry Jesus' cross.[50] |

---

[48] This line is not in Mark's text, so could be omitted: but something like it is surely implied by Mark 15.21.

## Act III – In and around Jerusalem

**Evangelist 1:** *(continuing)* And they bring Jesus to the place called Golgotha.

**Evangelist 2:** Which means, "The Place of a Skull".

*Rattle*

**Evangelist 1:** They offered him drugged wine.

**Soldier:** *(not unkindly)* Here lad, drink it. You won't feel so much. No? Well, if you won't, you won't.[51]

*Drumbeat*

**Evangelist 2.** Then they crucified him.

*Drumbeat*

They divided his clothes among them, throwing lots to decide what each should take.

*Drumbeat*

**Evangelist 1.** It was nine in the morning when they crucified him.

**Evangelist 2:** And the inscription of the charge against him read, 'The King of the Jews.'

*Drumbeat*

**Evangelist 1:** With him they crucified two bandits, one on his right and one on his left.

---

[49] Apparently Simon and Rufus are known to Mark's community. Mark is the only evangelist who mentions them. Rufus could, moreover, be the Rufus mentioned by Paul in connection with the Roman church at Romans 16.13. "The account does not encourage any speculation on the feelings of Simon, but it is natural to wonder whether this experience led to his converson" (Cranfield, *Mark* 454).

[50] It was normal for a condemned man to carry his own cross, but if Jesus had already received the preliminary flogging ordered by Pilate, he was perhaps too much weakened to be capable of it.

[51] For this direct form of what is evidently implied at Mark 15.23, I must acknowledge my indebtedness to Dorothy Sayers' *Man Born to be King* (301).

| | |
|---|---|
| **Evangelist 2.** | Those who passed by jeered at him! |
| **Passersby:** | *(various voices, male and female)* Save yourself, mate! |
| | You want to destroy the temple and build it in three days?!—save yourself! |
| | Come down from the cross! |
| | Come down from the cross, Messiah! |
| | That's right! Why don't you do that?! |
| **Evangelist 2:** | Then there were the chief priests and their scribes. |
| **Priests:** | *(various male voices, with clerical and academic pomposity)* He saved others—he cannot save himself! |
| | Come down from the cross, O Messiah, King of Israel! |
| | We will see and believe! *(clerical laughter)* |
| **Evangelist 2:** | Even those who were crucified with him taunted him. |
| **Crucified man:** | Save yourself and us, messiah![52] |
| **Evangelist 1:** | When it was noon, darkness came over the whole land until three in the afternoon. At three o'clock Jesus cried out, |
| **Jesus:** | *(in a loud voice)* Eloi, Eloi, lema sabachthani? My God, my God, why have you forsaken me? |
| **Bystanders** | *(various voices, this time curious):* |
| | Listen! He's shouting! |
| | He's calling for Elijah. |

---

[52] Again, this line (taken from Luke 23.39) is not in Mark's text, so the director may choose to omit it: but—as Luke evidently thought—something to this effect is surely implied by Mark 15.32?

## Act III – In and around Jerusalem

**Centurion:** Give him a drink, poor beggar.[53]

**Evangelist 2:** Someone ran and filled a sponge with sour wine. They put it on a stick and gave it to drink.

**Bystanders** *(various voices):* Wait!

Maybe Elijah will come!

And take him down?

Maybe!

**Evangelist 2:** Then Jesus gave a loud cry and breathed his last.

*Drumbeat.*

*Pause.*

**Evangelist 1:** And the curtain of the temple was torn in two from top to bottom.

*Drumbeat*

**Evangelist 1:** The centurion who stood facing him saw how he died.

**Centurion:** Truly, this man was a Son of God!

*Chime*

---

[53] Another line that is not in Mark's text, so the director may choose to omit it. But, again, I think it is what Mark intends us to understand by the episode, and it surely accords with the Centurion's final reaction to Jesus' death at Mark at 15.39. The giving of "sour wine" (contrary to "explanations" of it that I have occasionally heard from ill-informed preachers) was neither cruel or punitive. The "sour wine" that was offered will have been someone's own cooling drink: it was cheap, and common fare among soldiers and ordinary people generally. There is no reason to deny, and it indeed fits with the entire irony of the gospel—as well as being how the evangelist John appears to have understood this episode (see John 19.28-30)—that amid all the cruel mockery and brutal treatment that Jesus received, someone offered him a gesture of compassion. And why not someone among those from whom it might have been be least expected, i.e. the soldiers?—although, once again, I must confess I owe that last thought to Dorothy Sayers (*Man Born to be King* 309).

| | |
|---|---|
| **Evangelist 2:** | There were also women watching from a distance; among them were Mary Magdalene, and Mary the mother of James the younger and Joses, and Salome. These used to follow Jesus and provided for him when he was in Galilee. And there were many other women who had come up with him to Jerusalem. |
| | *Chime* |
| **Evangelist 1:** | When evening had come, and since it was the day of Preparation, that is, the day before the sabbath, Joseph of Arimathea, a respected member of the council, who was also himself waiting expectantly for the kingdom of God, went boldly to Pilate and asked for the body of Jesus. |
| **Pilate:** | *(surprised)* The prisoner is already dead?[54] So soon? Centurion, is this true? |
| **Centurion:** | Yes, sir. He barely lasted three hours. |
| **Pilate:** | I see. *(pause)* Well in that case—Joseph of Arimathea,[55] I assign the corpse to you. See to it according to your customs. |
| | *Drumbeat* |
| **Evangelist 2:** | Then Joseph bought a linen cloth, and taking down the body, wrapped it in the cloth and laid it in a tomb hewn out of the rock. He then rolled a stone against the entrance to the tomb. |

---

[54] Crucifixion was not, in general, a means to a quick death: nor was it intended to be.

[55] "In that case... I assign": Mark's word "ἐδωρήσατο" (NRSV "he granted") (15.45) makes it clear that Pilate's assigning the corpse to Joseph is a favour granted in view of a particular circumstance—in this case, the early and verified death of the crucified—and in accord with Roman imperial practice, which was to respect local custom, so long as it did not clash with or subvert Rome's own *imperium*.

Act III – In and around Jerusalem

*Drumbeat*

**Evangelist 2:** Mary Magdalene and Mary the mother of Joses saw where the body was laid.

*Drumbeat*

# Epilogue: The Resurrection of Jesus (Mark 16.1-8)[56]

| | |
|---|---|
| **Evangelist 2:** | When Sabbath was over, Mary Magdalene and Mary the mother of James and Salome bought spices, so they might go and anoint him. Very early on the first day of the week, just after sunrise, they went to the tomb. |
| **Salome:** | Who'll roll the stone away for us from the entrance? |
| **Mary, mother of James:** | Oh! Look! Mary! Look up there! |
| **Salome:** | The stone—it's huge! |
| **Mary Magdalen:** | Yes, yes, but don't you see? It's moved! It's already been rolled back! |
| | *Chime* |
| **Evangelist 2:** | They went in. And they saw a young man, wearing a white robe, sitting on the righthand side. They were alarmed!—but then: |
| **Angel:** | Do not be afraid! You seek Jesus of Nazareth, who was crucified. He has been raised. He is not here. Look where they laid him! But go, tell his disciples and Peter!—he is going ahead of you to Galilee. There you will see him, just as he told you. |

---

[56] According to all the best manuscripts, Mark's gospel ends here. For discussion and interpretation of the ending of the gospel, see my discussion, "The Ending to Mark's Gospel," above, pp. 15-18.

# Select Bibliography

Bauckham, Richard A. *Jesus and the Eyewitnesses: The Gospels as Eyewitness Testimony*. Second edition. Grand Rapids, Michigan: W. B. Eerdmans, 2017.

Boring, Eugene. *Mark*. Louisville: Westminster John Knox, 2006

Bryan, Christopher. *A Preface to Mark: Notes on the Gospel in Its Literary and Cultural Settings.*. New York: Oxford University, 1993.

Bryan, Christopher. *Render to Caesar: Jesus, The Early Church, and the Roman Superpower*. New York: Oxford University, 2005.

Bryan, Christopher. *The Resurrection of the Messiah*. New York: Oxford University, 2011.

Burridge, Richard A. *What Are the Gospels?: A Comparison with Graeco-Roman Biography*. Waco, Texas: Baylor University 2018 (Cambridge University, 1992).

Cranfield, C. E. B. *The Gospel according to St Mark*. Cambridge, England: Cambridge University, 1959.

Dwyer, Timothy. *The Motif of Wonder in the Gospel of Mark*. JSNTSup 128. Sheffield: Sheffield Academic, 1996.

Lightfoot, R. H. *The Gospel Message of St Mark*. Oxford: Clarendon, 1950.

Otto, Rudolf. *The Idea of the Holy: An Inquiry into the non-rational factor in the idea of the divine and its relation to the rational*. John W. Harvey, transl. London: Oxford University, 1923.

Sayers, Dorothy, *The Man Born to be King*. London: Gollancz, 1943.

Steiner, George. *Real Presences*. London: Faber and Faber, 1989.

Taylor, Vincent. *The Gospel according to St Mark*. London: Macmillan, 1957.

# About the Author

Sometime Woodward Scholar of Wadham College, Oxford, Christopher Bryan is an Anglican priest, novelist, and academic, who taught at the School of Theology of the University of the South in Sewanee for many years. Now semi-retired (whatever that means), he and his wife Wendy live in Exeter. His novels include *Siding Star* (Diamond Press, 2012), which was named to Kirkus Reviews Best Books of 2013, *Peacekeeper* (Diamond Press, 2013), *Singularity* (Diamond Press, 2014), *A Habit of Death* (Diamond Press, 2015), *The Dogleg Murders* (Diamond Press, 2016), *Black Ops* (Diamond Press, 2017) and *Death at Sea* (Diamond Press 2019).

Bryan's academic studies include *A Preface to Mark* (Oxford University Press, 1993), *Render to Caesar: Jesus, the Early Church, and the Roman Superpower* (Oxford University Press, 2005), *The Resurrection of the Messiah* (Oxford University Press, 2011), the popular *And God Spoke* (Cowley, 2012) (which was among the books chosen as commended reading for the Bishops at the 2008 Lambeth Conference), *Listening to the Bible: The Art of Faithful Biblical Interpretation* (Oxford University Press, 2014), *Son of God: Reflections on a Tradition* (Oxford University Press, 2023), and *Mary of Nazareth: The Mother of Jesus as Remembered by The Earliest Christians* (Seabury, 2024).